I0461220

TRUMPET BLISS SERIES

# Thompson Flexibility Studies

## TRUMPET OR CORNET VOL. I

A COMPREHENSIVE METHOD OF STUDY IN LIP FLEXIBILITY FOR THE FIRST TIME BEGINNING TRUMPET PLAYER OR COMEBACK PLAYER.

KURT THOMPSON

TRUMPETSIZZLE.COM

# THOMPSON FLEXIBILITY STUDIES
## TRUMPET OR CORNET
## VOL I

### KURT THOMPSON
### TRUMPETSIZZLE.COM

Copyright © 2022 by Kurt Thompson and Trumpetsizzle.com. All rights reserved worldwide. No part of this publication may be replicated, redistributed, or given away in any form without the prior written consent of the author/publisher or the terms relayed to you herein. You may not upload or download this book in any form, nor may you offer it for download as a pdf or any other type of format under the deception of fair use. This book/media is not public domain nor does "fair use" or 'educational purposes" apply to this material.

This book and media is only for personal use.

You may contact Kurt Thompson at kurt@trumpetsizzle.com and request permission should you wish to include an excerpt from this book in a scholastic type presentation. Permission is not granted until you receive a positive, affirmative reply from Kurt Thompson.

# Best Format For Practicing

This book may be published in a variety of formats. The best two formats to get the most out of this book are the paperback format and the hardback format editions. The third format of this book that may have been published is the Ebook.

This book was written with a "hands-on" approach in mind. The student would be diligently practicing, keeping written records of dates, progress, metronome markings and perhaps even marking up certain parts of the exercises to further expedite progress along with efficiency.

The Ebook is not the full version of the book.

The paperback and hardback versions are the FULL version of the book and allow ample room for note taking. Further, as recommended in the book, your private trumpet teacher will enjoy the extra room where they can write helpful notes for you, the student, including dates, how long you have been working on a particular assignment, particular challenges you may be having, and etc...

The Ebook is a condensed version of the paperback and hardback editions. It contains some, but not all of the exercises and information. It also does not afford the student and/or teacher to write and make notes. Thus, the Ebook dampens the spirit of the Author's intent.

So, why is there an Ebook version? Cost is the big factor. The Ebook may very well be only 25% or less of the cost of the paperback version and certainly 25% or less of the cost of the hardback edition. For players on a budget or for trumpet players residing in countries that have a weaker currency than the dollar, the student may have no other choice but to purchase only the Ebook version.

The Ebook's content is as good as or better than some of the long standing methods that have been around for decades. In other words, it would be much better to purchase the Ebook version than nothing at all and certainly better than getting involved in many of the outdated, lesser quality method books that are out there.

Many younger, trumpet students in their teens and early twenties prefer most of their content in a digital format. After reading this information regarding the best format for this book, they may STILL prefer to purchase the Ebook version even knowing it is a condensed version and does not allow for note taking and markup while practicing through the book.

As the old American saying goes: "You can lead a horse to water, but you can't make them practice out of the paperback version!" hahaha....

Regardless of which format you choose to purchase, start practicing right away! Whether you turn on and power up your "book" or you physically take it off a desk or table and put it on your stand, START PRACTICING!

*Trumpet Bliss Series*

Thompson Flexibility Studies Vol. 1

...Stay tuned as more will be added soon

# Who Is This Book For?

This is Vol. 1 of the *Thompson Flexibility Studies* for trumpet players. It is designed for beginning trumpet players. It is also designed for players returning to the horn after a very long time of not playing or practicing. If you are an intermediate or advanced trumpet player, this volume will likely only be part of a good daily warm up for you. Why? If you are not a beginner or comeback player, it will be too easy.
So, if you ARE a beginner or comeback player, you are in the right place!

On the other hand, what if you are in 8th grade starting your 2nd or 3rd year of playing trumpet? What if you are a comeback player, but you actually restarted the trumpet a year ago or 2 years ago? Well, you may find this book easy. Perhaps you may find it too easy.

If you truly are an intermediate trumpet player or advanced, or if you are a comeback player who really isn't a comeback player anymore i.e. you have already been practicing everyday for the last year or more, this book at most will serve as a good part of your daily warm up. You should seriously consider starting Vol. II of the Thompson Flexibility Studies.

I want the right player to be using this book and having a good time doing so. I made this book such that a beginner doesn't even need to know all their fingerings or the name of the notes. All they have to do is understand the valve numbering system to play through most of these exercises. Having a basic understanding of note and rest values is also a requirement. (i.e. quarter note, whole rest, and etc...)

# How To Use This Book

As I just previously stated in the other section: 'I made this book such that a beginner doesn't even need to know all their fingerings or the name of the notes. All you have to do is understand the valve numbering system to play through these exercises'.

While we are on the subject, let's quickly review:

There are 3 trumpet valves (pistons) that one presses down while playing the trumpet. They actually pop up on their own. These 3 valves lengthen or shorten the tubing of the trumpet thus causing different pitches to come out of the bell of horn. There are many combinations.

What you need to know is that there are 3 valves and each is numbered. Yes, they are numbered! No, I am not joking. If you unscrew and take each valve out of the casing, you will notice either a 1, 2, or 3 depending on which valve you took out.

When you are holding the trumpet to play, the valve closest to you is valve NUMBER 1. The middle valve is valve NUMBER 2. The valve furthest away from you is valve NUMBER 3.

The code works like this: If you see "1" under a note or measure or entire line of notes, you hold down the 1st valve only.

Same thing if you see "2" under a note or measure.

What happens if you see this: 13? That is not 13. It really is 1 and 3. This means you need to press or hold down valves 1 and 3 at the same time.

What happens if you see 23 under a note, under a measure, bar, etc...? That is not 23, but really 2 and 3! It means you are supposed to press down valves 2 and 3 at the same time.

During this book you might see "0" underneath the first measure plus some dashes, but nothing else for the rest of that line. Then, on the next line you might see a "2" plus some dashes. What is going on here is that you are supposed to play all notes for each line with that valve or valve combination.

"0" at the beginning means to play all notes in an open position. Open position means don't push any valves down.

The same would be true for the next line if you see "2". You would only press the 2nd valve down.

Some exercises in this book have valve positions that change every measure or every few measures.

Don't worry. It should be obvious because the new valve combinations will be written right under the measure you are supposed to change valve positions.

The theme of this book is: DON'T TONGUE!

Lip Flexibility implies using your embouchure: the tension and relaxation of your lips to control the notes and also to control moving up or down in pitch. The speed of the air you blow through the horn is also a factor.

If you really think about the fact you might be playing 2 or more different notes, but not moving your valves and not tonguing, a feeling of confusion might wash over you.

It's ok.

At first, it may be a little frustrating or even a tad scary.

You can do it.

The very nature of this book and design has tilted the odds in your favor to begin playing and practicing your first lip slurs.

I have no doubt that you will certainly be able to do it.


Could there still be a problem even if you now know how to follow the valve system? Yes. If you don't know what a whole note is or a quarter rest, well, that presents a problem and goes back to my advice on having a teacher work with you through this book.

There is a silver lining...maybe even more than one!

I tend to make companion video tutorials for the lessons and courses I teach.

At the time of this writing, there is not one made, but please check my site, Trumpetsizzle.com, to see if I ended up making one.

In the back of my mind, I have an idea to make not only a video tutorial, but possibly a partial play along.

At the very least, I probably will play one example from each exercise which would definitely point you in the right direction.

What is the other silver lining?

Youtube!

There are so many beginning music theory videos right now on youtube that it is quite likely you could find one just for you. A beginning music theory video will go over the lines and spaces of the staff, time signature, note and rest values plus a whole lot more. Please look into a good highly rated music theory video for beginners.

If Youtube is no longer around and you have never heard of it, I bet you can probably find the popular video sharing platform that took its place.


The metronome.

It is critical that you use the metronome each and every time you practice with this book.

The metronome keeps the beat for you.

The metronome keeps you honest.

How does it keep you honest?

Players tend to slow down when they encounter harder sections and speed up during the easier sections.

The metronome will make it very obvious if you slow down or speed up.

You can have a stand alone quartz metronome. You may also have a wind up metronome. A digital metronome from an app is also perfectly fine. The main point is to have your metronome ready for action when you start practicing in this book.

Most books that I have seen do a disservice to the student when they present an exercise that has a metronome marking that looks like this:

Exercise 52 m.m. 96-120

Does that mean you should at least be able to play it at 96 before moving on? Does it mean that 120 is the green light and THEN you can move on to the next exercise?

It provides a lot of ambiguity for the student and most will just shoot for the slower number of the two or sometimes split the difference in the middle.

This book is direct. There is no ambiguity when it comes to the speed of an exercise. Several of the exercises are graded with increases in speed.

Let's take Exercise. 19 in this book as an example. In the first slow version, you will see m.m. 60. You are to practice this one until you can cleanly play all lines and all valve combinations without any mistakes. 60 is quite slow so many of you might be able to knock this one out in the first day or two.

Great!

If you master Exercise 19 at 60, you are not done.

Move on to the next exercise in the book, but guess what? The next exercise is still Exercise 19, but...at a faster tempo!

Exercise 19 at m.m. 80 is the medium version.

Repeat the same strategy as above and once you can play through the entire exercise cleanly and with no mistakes, move on to the next exercise.

Guess what?

The next exercise is still Exercise 19, but yet at a faster tempo again.

The third version of Exercise 19 is medium fast with a metronome m.m. tempo of 100.

Yes, m.m. 100 is moving along at a good clip and you won't just sail through this version like you did the first version which was a slow m.m. 60.

It will take you longer, but whenever you arrive at the point where you can play Exercise 19 at 100 with no problems, guess what?

You know the drill: There is one last version of Exercise 19 and it is to be played at a blistering fast tempo of m.m. = 120. Yikes!

You can do it!

Be patient.

This one will take even more time to conquer, but it is possible as long as you don't give up. Keep working it day by day and at some point, you will be able to play it cleanly all the way through.

Don't worry: Not every exercise has 4 versions. Some have none. Some have only two versions.

Having some of the exercises graded by increasing the metronome speed takes away the anxiety and ambiguity.

You don't have to wonder which tempo is the magic tempo that proves you have succeeded.

In this book the metronome marking and tempo is written in stone for each exercise and for each version of the same exercise. You either can play it at the stated tempo and are able to move on OR you must continue practicing that specific version until you have achieved that stated speed.

When I use the term "graded", I am using it similar to a grade that shows how steep an incline is. Sometimes on a highway, you might see a sign that says:

Steep 11% grade ahead. Trucks use the right lane only.

Now, does that make it a bit more clear in regards to the word "grade"?

Hopefully it does.

Let's have some fun!

See you in Exercise Number One!

Kurt Thompson

September 2022

# Introduction

First things first: This trumpet exercise book is for true beginners and true comeback players. If you have been playing trumpet solidly for 2-3 years, this book might be too easy for you. If you are not a true comeback player, meaning a player who actually returned to the horn 1 or 2 years ago after several decades of not playing, but who has been playing just about every day for the last year or more, this book might be too easy for you.

You are no longer a true comeback player if you have been playing solidly for several years in a row. At that point, you are officially back in the ranks as a bonafide trumpet player with no "comeback" in front of the word trumpet.

You are a true comeback player when, after several years or several decades of not playing, you decide to take action. Maybe you buy a trumpet because you haven't had one for decades. Maybe you send in your old ax to be reconditioned. At the point you have a trumpet in hand for the first time in years and you are about to put that mouthpiece and trumpet up to your lips and play, yes, you are a true comeback player at that moment!

If you got this book, but did find it too easy, guess what? It makes a perfect part of your warmup!

Guess what else?

There is a Vol.II from the Thompson Flexibility Studies for you and I guarantee that Vol. II will be a serious challenge for you to undertake!

As a younger, budding trumpet player, I always hated 2 things about most trumpet exercise books in those days:

- Print was too small to read easily

- Notes were too small and all packed in like sardines

I did have bad eyesight and was always quite nearsighted. Barely being able to read and play things like Arban's Carnival of Venice was hard enough, but when you factor in that everything was jammed up close and tight into a couple of pages, it just made things very tough on me.

As a result of my bad experiences with quite a whole lot of trumpet method and exercise books in my past, I have vowed to make my books:

- Easier to read with much larger print
- Notes easier to read and not all jammed together

In my new series, *Trumpet Bliss*, I truly believe I have achieved a very easy to read and play group of method books!

Heck, everything is large and clear enough that it just may be possible to read and practice these books in the very late afternoon or early evening with no lamps turned on in your living room or practice area!

Trumpet has so many facets to consider, to learn, to practice, to master, or at least attempt to master that it would be outside the scope of this book to address them all.

Techniques like *"Tongue Arch"* and *"Roll-in, Roll-out"*, and of course *"Compression Breathing"* need to be learned and understood, but THAT is where your private trumpet teacher comes in handy.

Therefore, I highly recommend you work with a professional while going through this book and any other books in the *Trumpet Bliss* series. They will be able to go in deep with you regarding some of the techniques previously mentioned.

It is possible to learn them on your own. I did. It was not easy for me nor was it efficient. A good professional trumpet teacher can save you time and your hair. Yes, you won't get so frustrated going it alone that you end up pulling out all your hair.

Taking lessons will allow you to become a great trumpeter plus allow you to keep all your hair and most of your sanity!

All kidding aside, go ahead and get started in this book, but do keep in mind that having a qualified trumpet professional looking out for you is not a bad idea.

When I was a very young student, I was always too excited to get started playing in any new trumpet book that I got. Whether it be Herbert L. Clarke's *Technical Studies* or Charles Colin's *Advanced Lip Flexibilities* or Claude Gordon's *Systematic Approach To Daily Practice*, I was always in a hurry.

Don't get me wrong: I did eventually go back and read their introductions and sometimes long lectures on trumpet pedagogy, but initially, I was too excited and had to jump right in to playing some of the exercises.

There also was this problem: Even after reading what they wrote, I didn't fully understand it all. Maybe it was because I was 13 years old taking a look at my first Herbert L. Clarke book or maybe it was because I was 16 years old just starting out in Charles Colin's lip trill book for the first time and really did not have the experience and maturity to understand everything they were talking about.

I have made most of my *Trumpet Bliss* series of study more like a workbook. I would prefer you have a teacher involved. With each exercise, I have left a place for you to make notes and also, hopefully, your teacher too.

At the very least, dates with metronome markings should be written in this section. That will keep you honest!

I could probably write a 50 page book or more just on lip flexibility and how to execute them properly. From tongue arch, to how to approach glissandos vs. lip trills, to how long you should spend on each exercise before moving to the next exercise and on and on and on...

But, I won't do that because what I have done instead is to add a set of instructions for each exercise as you go through the book. In the aforementioned books of trumpet study, most of their instruction happened at the beginning, but what happens to the student when they are 8, 10, or 20 pages away from the beginning? Most students will not keep flipping back and forth in a trumpet exercise book to refresh their mind on the author's opinions and instructions. So, by having instructions immediately preceding each new exercise, the end result will be better efficiency.

If you skimmed or skipped all the way to right here and didn't read my preceding words of wisdom (hehe), then let me give you some pointers you *must* do while practicing through this book:

- ☐ Learn tongue arch
- ☐ Learn roll-in and roll-out
- ☐ Play most of the exercises softly and relaxed
- ☐ Do not short change the rests in each exercise
- ☐ Rest 3-4 minutes after you have completed one exercise before moving onto something else in your daily practice routine.
- ☐ Obey the metronome markings
- ☐ Mark and date which exercise you are practicing and the current metronome marking (speed) you have achieved to date
- ☐ Don't skip a day of practicing. Find a way to practice every day. Yes, that means in the evenings if you have to and on the weekends.
- ☐ Leave your horn out on a trumpet stand 24/7 instead of having it stuck inside your case when you are not practicing.
- ☐ Be ready to move on to the next book in the *Trumpet Bliss* series and/or move up to the next level i.e. beginning to intermediate or intermediate to advanced.

I suppose there is one more pointer: Please try to get with a professional trumpet instructor who will definitely make things a lot easier on your journey. If you are a young teen or even younger, finding someone local in your area so that you may have your lessons in person is the way to go. If this is not possible, find someone that teaches remotely or online.

As of the date of this book's publication, I am still teaching a variety of trumpet and brass lessons at all levels and from all walks of life. As long as I haven't joined Maynard Ferguson, Rafael Mendez, Maurice Andre, and many others in the Heaven's Street Jazz Band, you may always reach out to me via my site, Trumpetsizzle.com.

If you can't find a convenient schedule with me, then please keep trying to find someone else. You won't regret working with someone who has already been where you are because there are just way too many areas of trumpet where you can be helped for me to list here, but trust me, working with a professional private teacher is the way to go to get the best results for yourself.

You are now about to embark on a fun-filled journey starting with Vol. 1 of the *Thompson Flexibility Studies*.

Enjoy!

Kurt Thompson

# Comments and Suggestions for Exercise 1

You should tongue the very first note of a slur which in this case starts on a G whole note. You tongue the G. Hold the G for 4 beats, then drop (or fall) into the low C. Do not tongue the low C.

As a beginner or comeback player, your goal is to be able to play both notes all in one breath. When you drop (or fall) into the low C which is the 2nd note, you want to move quickly and cleanly down doing your best to avoid hitting that elusive speed bump that is inherent in almost all flexibility endeavors on the trumpet.

Think of the speed bump as similar to air turbulence while traveling in an airplane. Up in the sky, you truly are not hitting a physical object, but you can surely feel it when the plane encounters turbulence.

So, your goal is to minimize this "turbulence" or speed bump and proceed cleanly and quickly to the note you are slurring to.

These are played mp which means mezzo piano or medium soft.

Use your metronome. In fact, the metronome is non-negotiable for most of the exercises you will encounter in this flexibility book.

Obey all rests. This requires patience as many players will want to skip the rests and jump right to the next playing part.

When you have finished playing all of Exercise 1, make sure to rest for at least 3-5 minutes. Put the horn down. Resting means you no longer have the trumpet touching the lips. It also means you are doing nothing at all with your lips or tongue i.e. no buzzing, no tonguing, etc...

## Teacher or Student Notes:

# Exercise 1

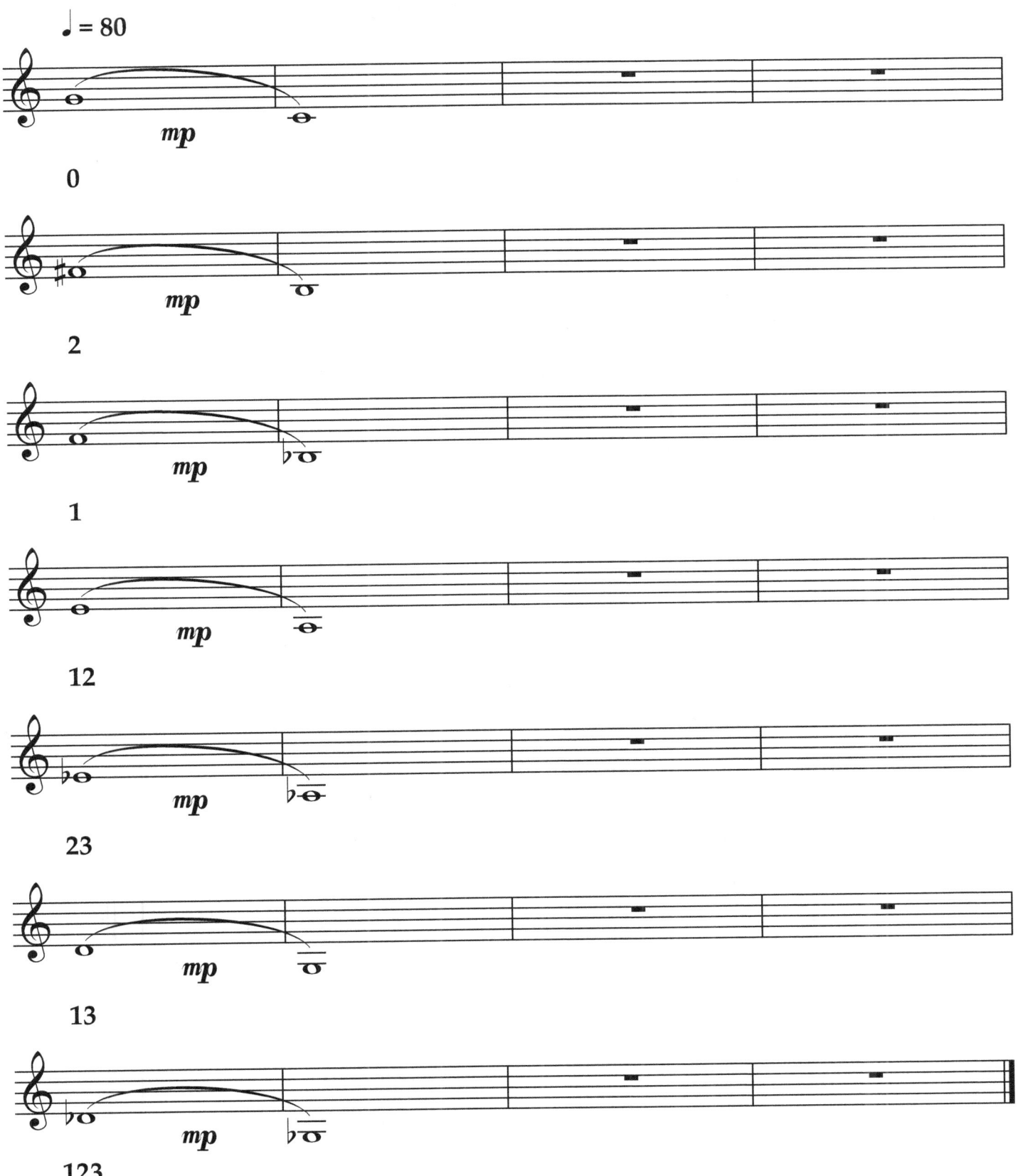

# Comments and Suggestions for Exercise 2

You will notice right away that exercise 2 presents a challenge. The challenge is slurring up to a note. This requires more embouchure (lip muscle) strength.

It also requires faster moving air and for you to employ the tongue positioning: "AH" to "EE".

It could be possible that you aren't able to play the very first 2 measures. It is ok.

Rest 5-10 seconds then try again. If after 3-5 attempts, you aren't having any success, please stop and rest 3-5 minutes before making any more attempts.

If you had trouble with Exercise 2 and you took your 5 minute rest, do not repeatedly attempt to hammer away at Exercise 2. Try it only a few more times then stop for this practice day.

You can always begin tomorrow stronger and rested which might increase your odds of success!

When you have finished playing all of Exercise 2, make sure to rest for at least 3-5 minutes. Put the horn down. Resting means you no longer have the trumpet touching the lips. It also means you are doing nothing at all with your lips or tongue i.e. no buzzing, no tonguing, etc...

Quick Takeaway: Use a metronome. Obey all rests. Obey the dynamic marking i.e. mp, mf, f, which indicate how loud or soft you should play. For Exercise 2 you will be playing medium soft (mp).

Don't forget: When playing from low to high, use Tongue Arch ("AH" to "EE") tongue positioning. Your private teacher is the best person to guide you learning and using tongue arch.

Teacher or Student Notes:

# Exercise 2

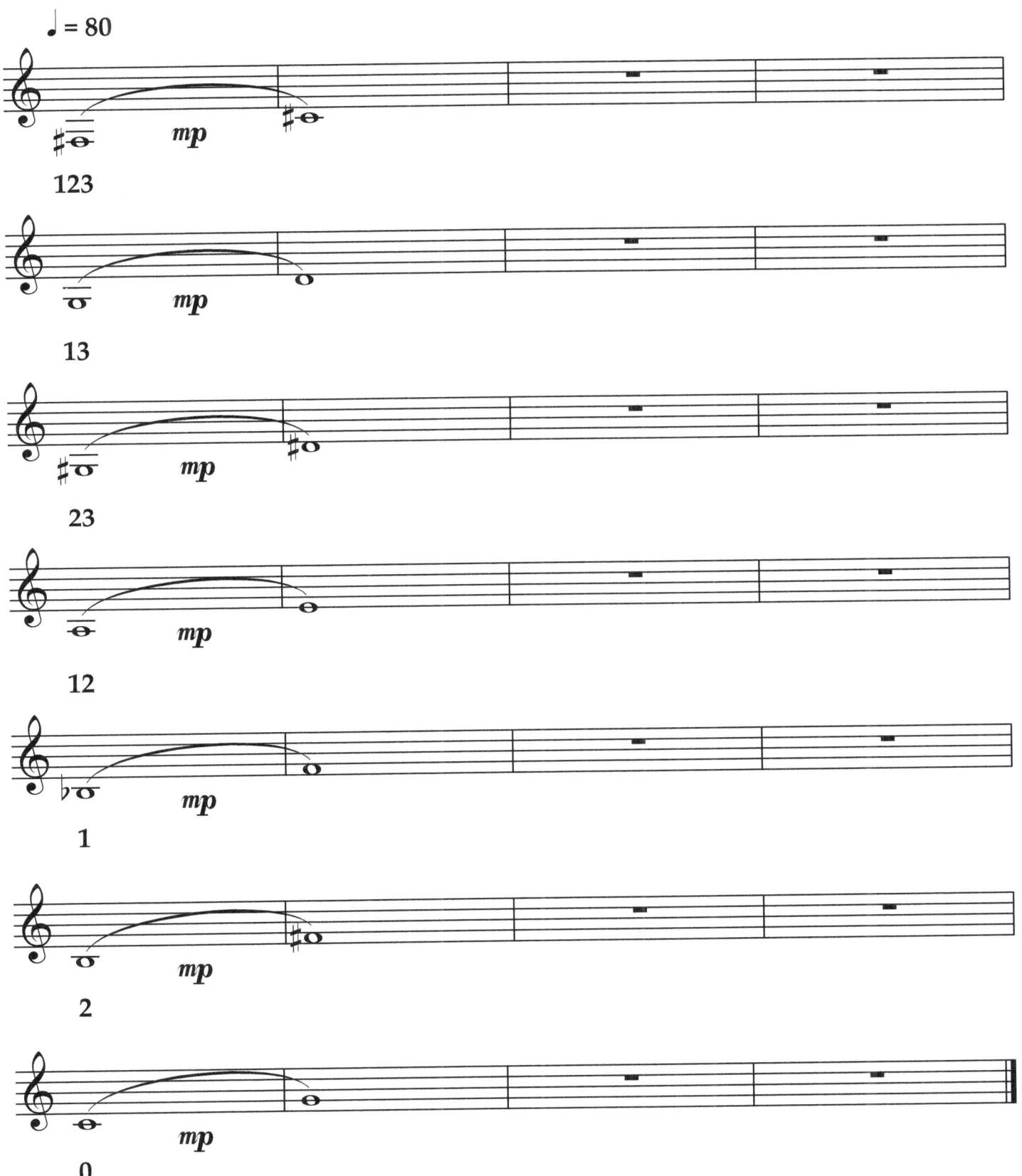

# Comments and Suggestions for Exercise 3

In this exercise you will begin moving a bit quicker. No, we didn't change the metronome speed. Notice you are now playing half notes not whole notes. You have to think fast. You have 2 beats to plan your move, not 4 beats as in the previous 2 exercises.

The entire exercise is medium soft - mp.

Set the metronome and count those rests!

## Teacher or Student Notes:

# Exercise 3

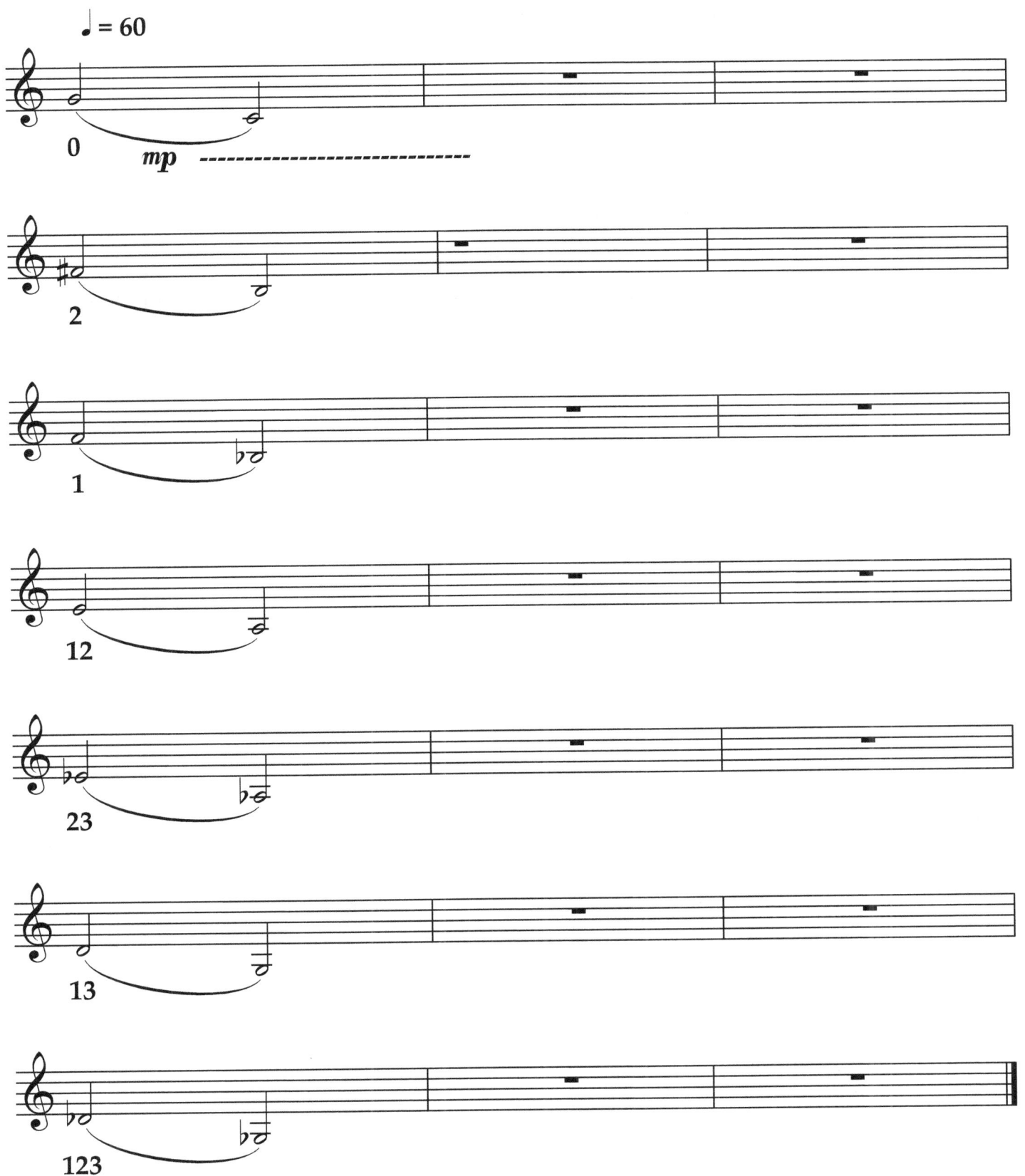

# Comments and Suggestions for Exercise 4

In this exercise you will begin moving a bit quicker like you did in Exercise 3. Don't forget: When slurring from a low note to a higher note, you will need to make sure your tongue is in "AH" position to begin with and then your tongue moves in to "EE" position to "pop" the higher note to come out. Put the horn down and say: "AH - EE". Do that a few times because when we employ this tongue position while playing the trumpet, we REALLY are doing this. The tongue actually is moving. We aren't thinking "AH -EE", but instead are physically causing the tongue to move up and down. The tip of the tongue does NOT move! The tip of the tongue stays anchored (attached or fixed) behind the lower teeth.

The entire exercise is medium soft - mp.

Set the metronome and count those rests!

## Teacher or Student Notes:

# Exercise 4

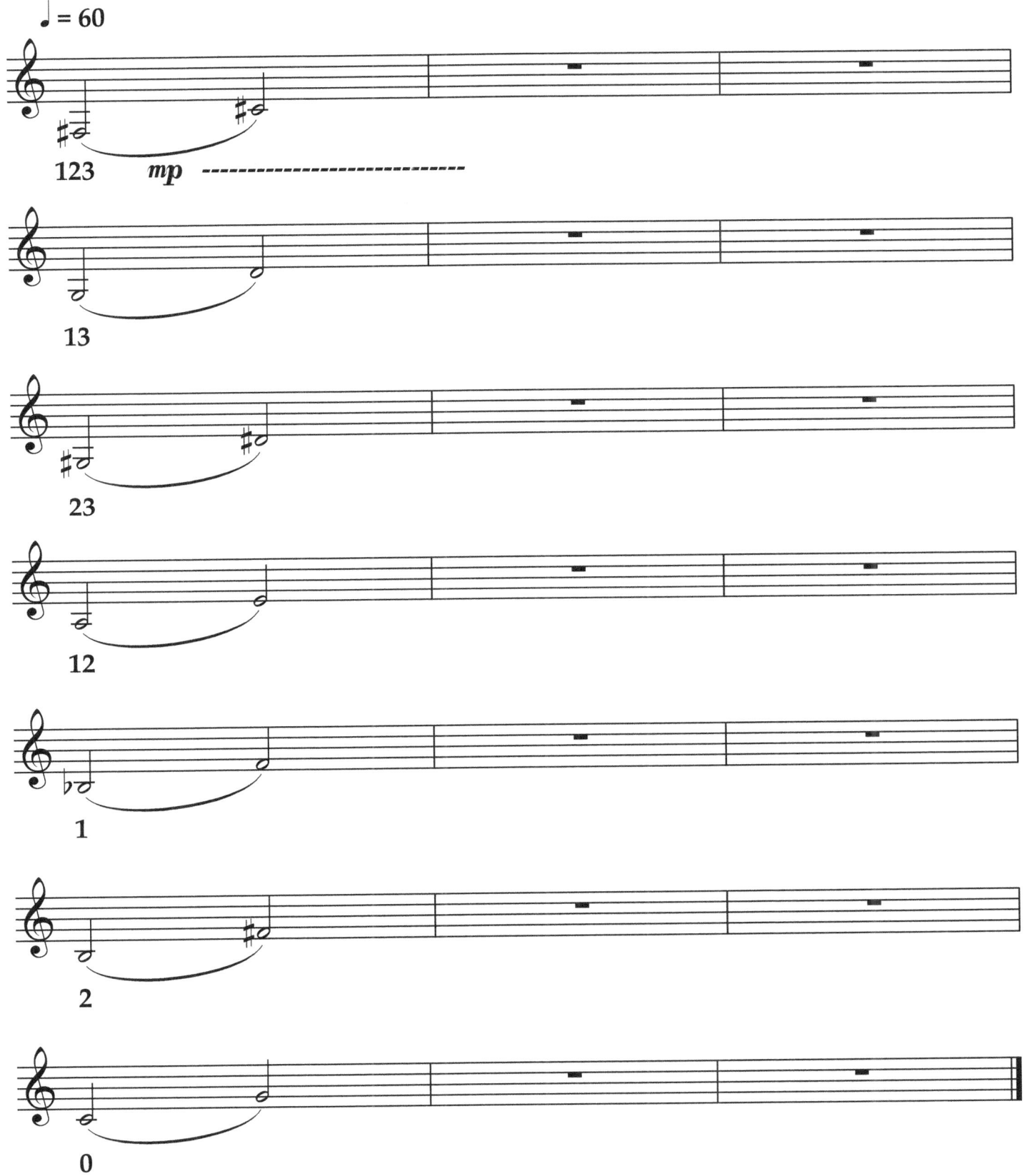

# Comments and Suggestions for Exercise 5

In this exercise you will begin moving a bit quicker because the metronome actually changes to a faster speed: 72. We also have added a note so now you have 3 notes to contend with. You can do it! Be aware that on the second note your tongue must be in "AH" position and getting ready to move up to "EE" position so you can get that third note to lock in easily and smoothly.

The entire exercise is medium soft - mp.

Set the metronome and count those rests!

## Teacher or Student Notes:

# Exercise 5

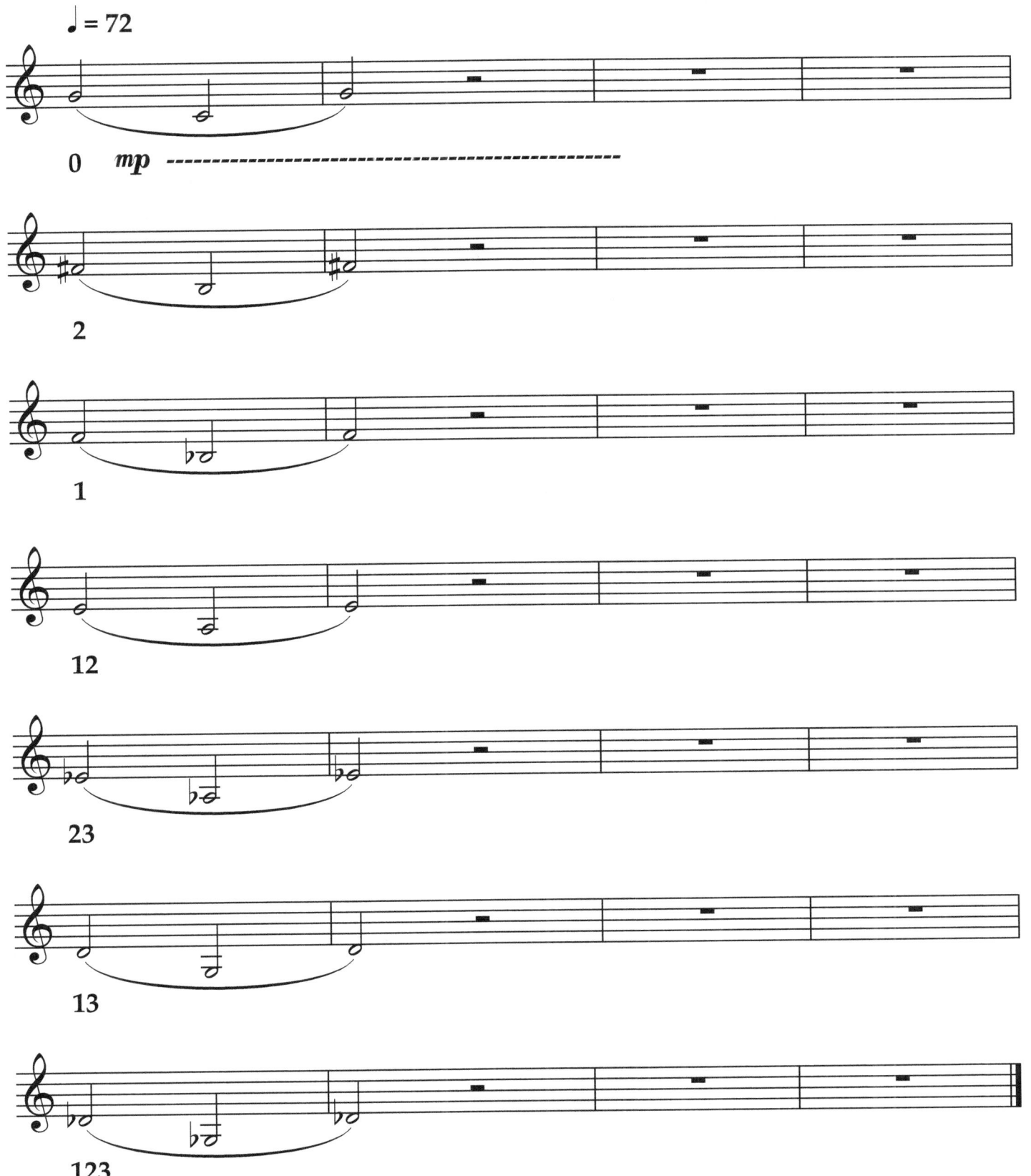

# Comments and Suggestions for Exercise 6

You can use the same information and directions from Exercise 5 for this one. ('We also have added a note so now you have 3 notes to contend with. Be aware that on the first note, your tongue must be in "AH" position and getting ready to move up to "EE" position so you can get that second note to lock in easily and smoothly.')

The metronome is also the same at 72.

The entire exercise is medium soft - mp.

Set the metronome and count those rests!

## Teacher or Student Notes:

# Exercise 6

# Comments and Suggestions for Exercise 7

We have added another note so now there are 4 notes to play before you rest. Did you notice the slur does not cover all 4 notes, but only 2 at a time? This means the first note in the second measure of every line is tongued.

Yes, the actual speed has increased. Please notice the metronome should be set to 80.

Do your best to play all the notes in one breath.

The entire exercise is medium soft - mp.

Set the metronome and count those rests!

## Teacher or Student Notes:

# Exercise 7

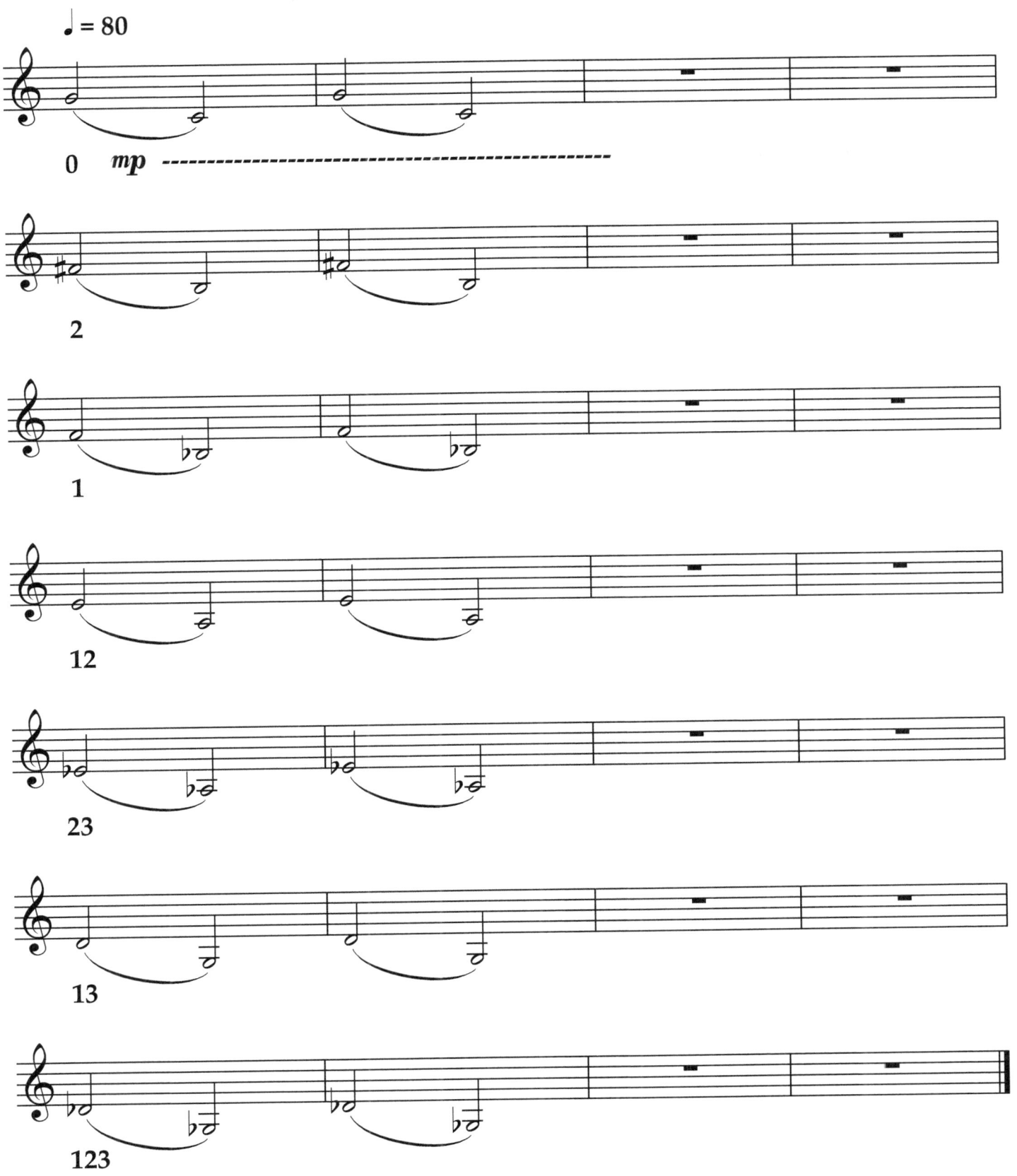

# Comments and Suggestions for Exercise 8

The same directions you followed for Exercise 7 can also be applied here in Exercise 8.
The entire exercise is medium soft - mp.
Set the metronome and count those rests!

## Teacher or Student Notes:

# Exercise 8

# Comments and Suggestions for Exercise 9

Be ready! Notes are moving more quickly.

The entire exercise is medium soft - mp.

Set the metronome and count those rests!

## Teacher or Student Notes:

# Exercise 9

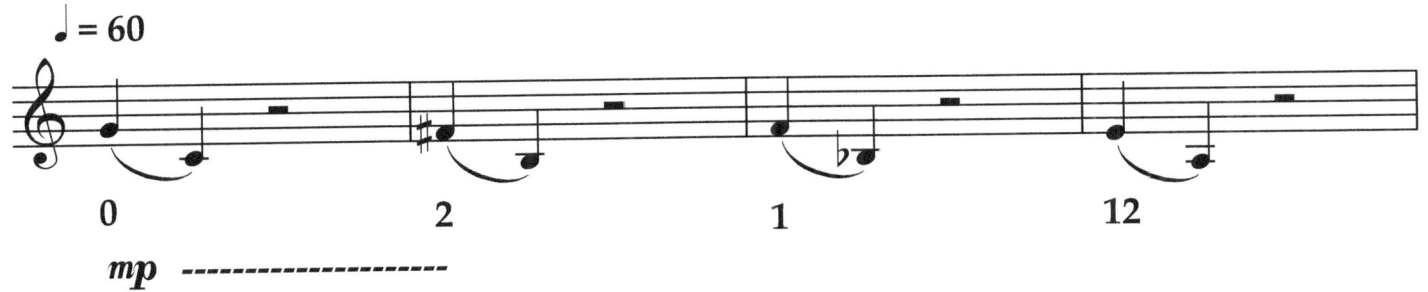

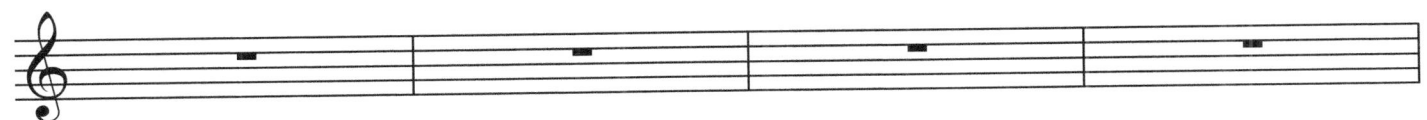

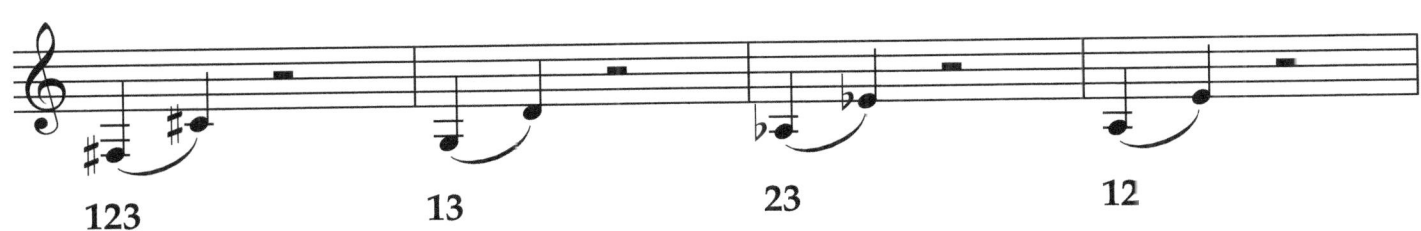

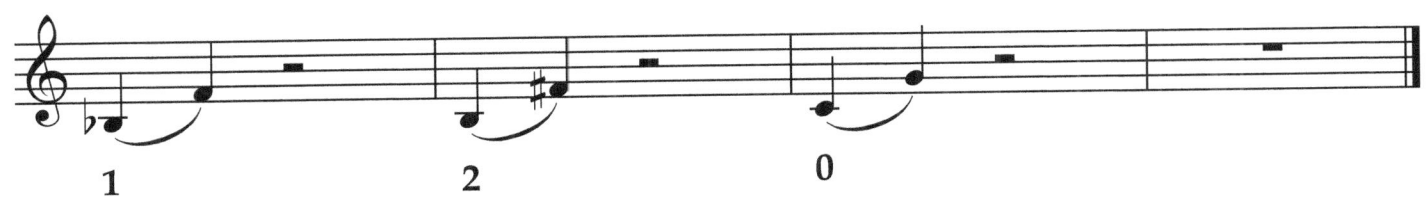

# Comments and Suggestions for Exercise 9 (faster)

You must set the metronome to 80. Concentrate.

Obey all rests.

The entire exercise is medium soft - mp.

## Teacher or Student Notes:

# Exercise 9 (faster)

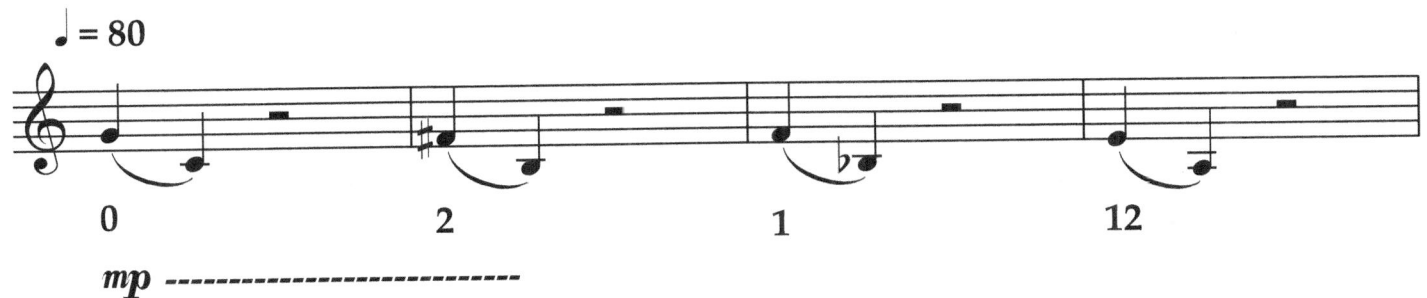

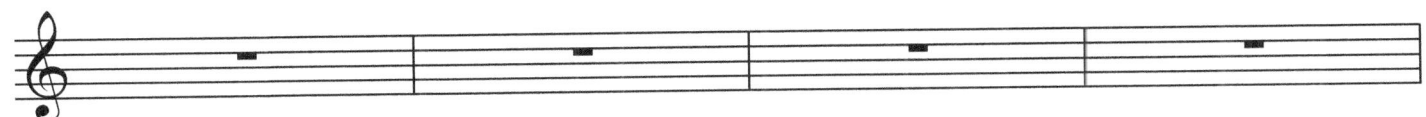

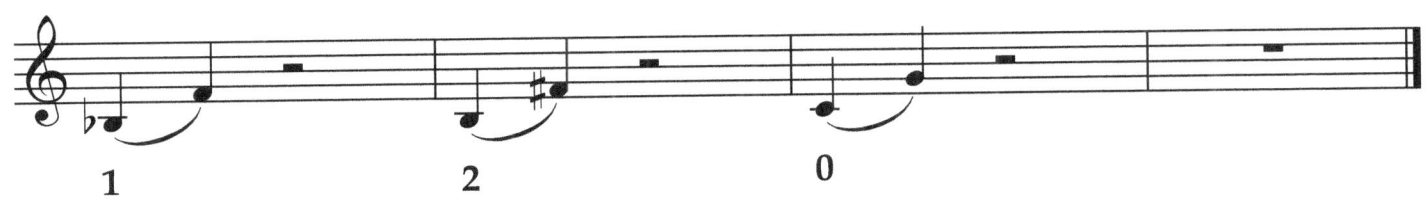

# Comments and Suggestions for Exercise 10

Notice the change in articulation from slurring to tonguing. When you tongue the tenuto notes, try to tongue as lightly as possible to make them sound almost slurred. The tenuto notes are the notes with a dash line under them.

The entire exercise is medium soft - mp.

Set the metronome and count those rests!

## Teacher or Student Notes:

# Exercise 10

# Comments and Suggestions for Exercise 10 (faster)

You must set the metronome to 80.

Obey all rests.

The entire exercise is medium soft - mp.

Teacher or Student Notes:

# Exercise 10 (faster)

# Comments and Suggestions for Exercise 11

Be alert for the alternating articulation: Slurring, Tenuto. Also, when you have 2 notes slurred then another 2 notes slurred, you don't slur all. You tongue the first note of each slur. For example: In the first measure, you will tongue the G on beat one and then tongue the G again on beat two.

The entire exercise is medium soft - mp.

Set the metronome and count those rests!

## Teacher or Student Notes:

# Exercise 11

45

# Comments and Suggestions for Exercise 11 (faster)

You must set the metronome to 80.

Obey all rests.

The entire exercise is medium soft - mp.

## Teacher or Student Notes:

# Exercise 11 (faster)

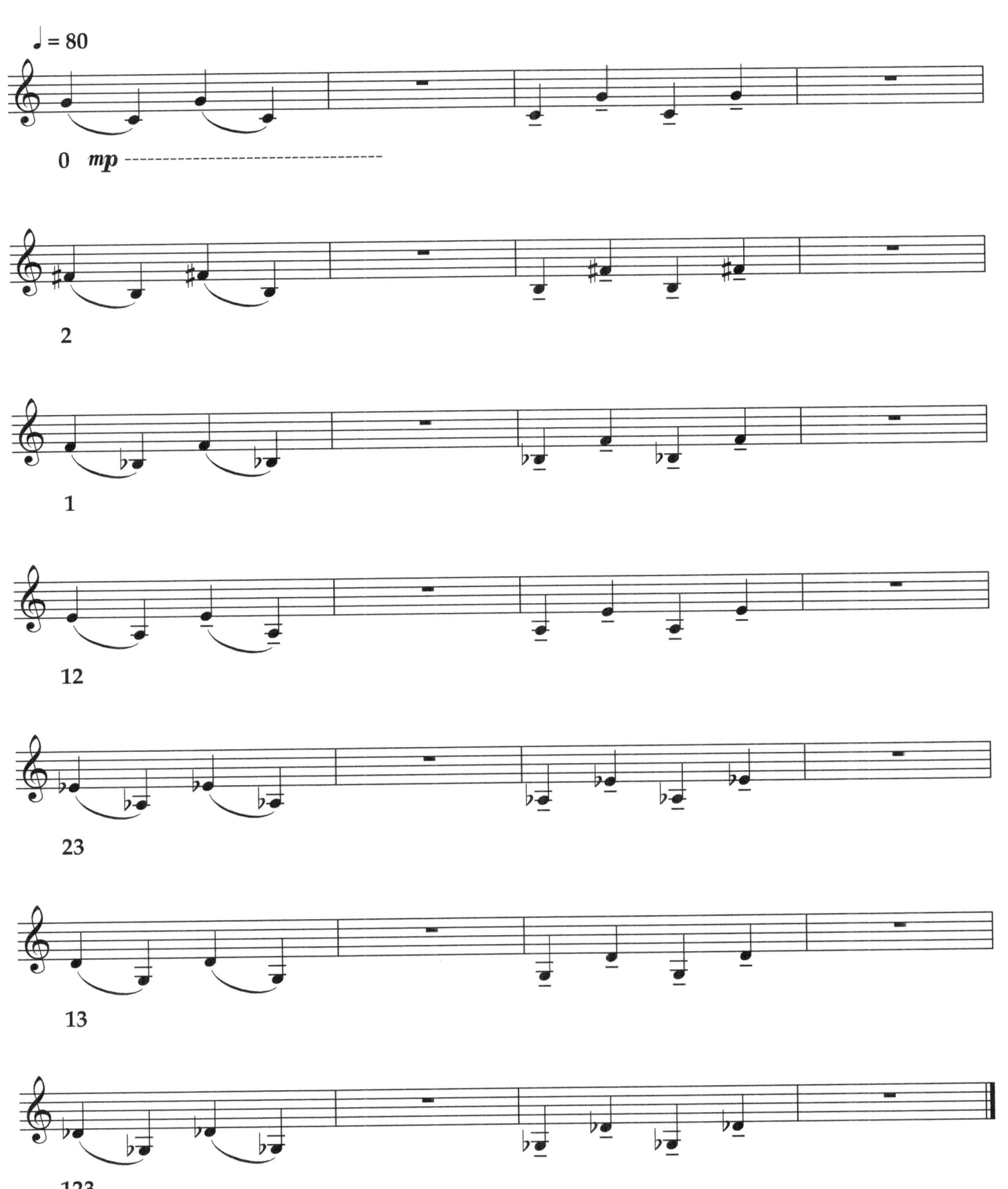

# Comments and Suggestions for Exercise 12

Be alert for the alternating articulation: Slurring, Tenuto. When you are tonguing tenuto, try to make the notes so smooth and so lightly attacked that it almost sounds like you are slurring!

The entire exercise is medium soft - mp.

Set the metronome and count those rests!

## Teacher or Student Notes:

# Exercise 12

# Comments and Suggestions for Exercise 12 (faster)

You must set the metronome to 80.

Obey all rests.

The entire exercise is medium soft - mp.

## Teacher or Student Notes:

# Exercise 12 (faster)

# Comments and Suggestions for Exercise 13

Notice that you are now playing more without being able to rest. That's ok because you now have better endurance!

The entire exercise is medium soft - mp.

Set the metronome and count those rests!

## Teacher or Student Notes:

# Exercise 13

# Comments and Suggestions for Exercise 13 (faster)

You must set the metronome to 80.

Obey all rests.

The entire exercise is medium soft - mp.

## Teacher or Student Notes:

# Exercise 13 (faster)

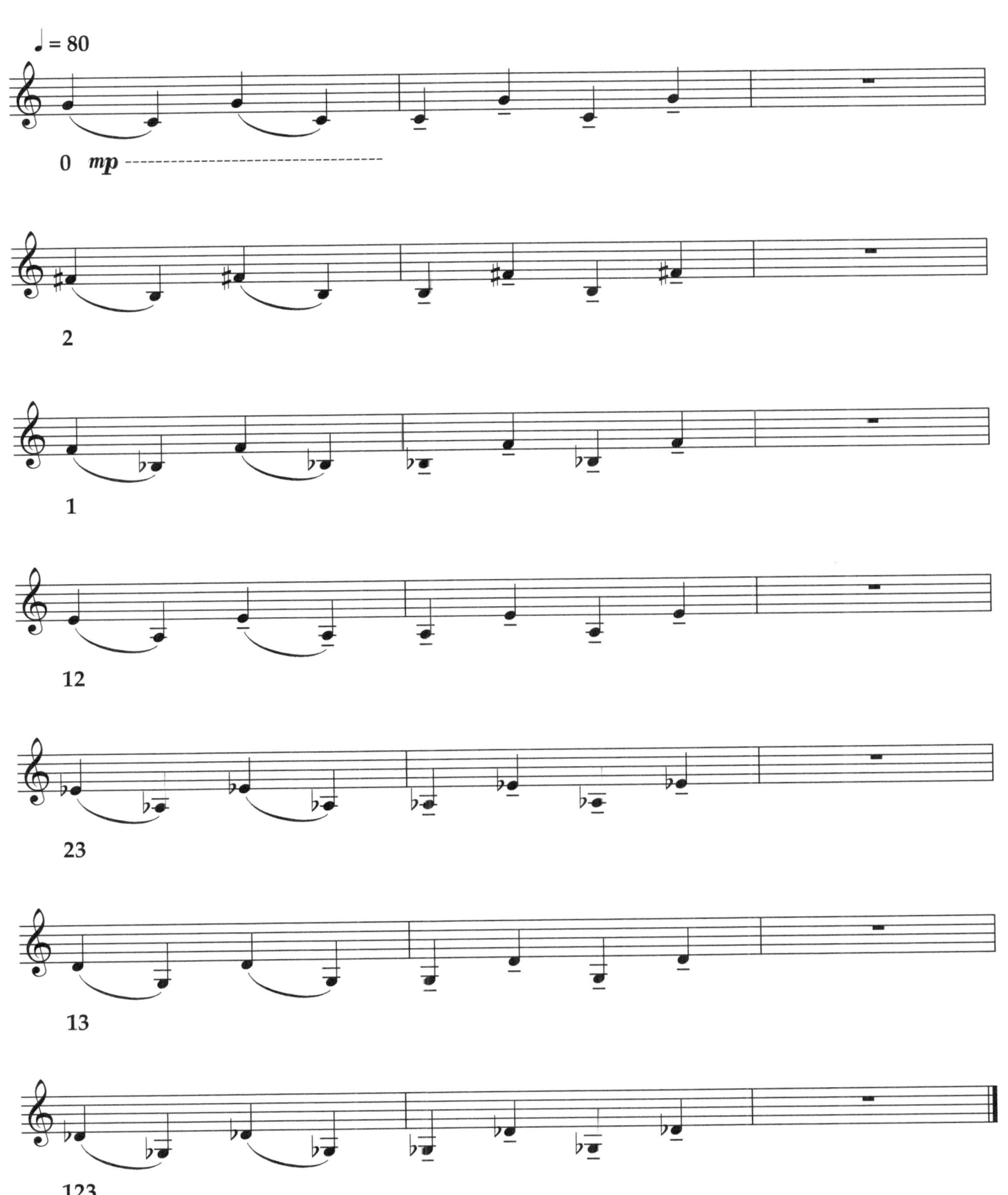

# Comments and Suggestions for Exercise 14

The entire exercise is medium soft - mp.
Set the metronome and count those rests!

## Teacher or Student Notes:

# Exercise 14

# Comments and Suggestions for Exercise 14 (faster)

You must set the metronome to 80.

Obey all rests.

The entire exercise is medium soft - mp.

## Teacher or Student Notes:

# Exercise 14 (faster)

59

# Comments and Suggestions for Exercise 15

Stop! Look! Concentrate!

Notice the articulation is different for each line. Notice that the valve combinations change twice a measure. Yikes, but you can do it! If m.m. 60 is too fast, try without the metronome for a few times until you get used to the fast valve changes.

However, as soon as you get comfortable, make sure to turn that metronome back on at 60 and try to get it!

The entire exercise is medium soft - mp.

## Teacher or Student Notes:

# Exercise 15

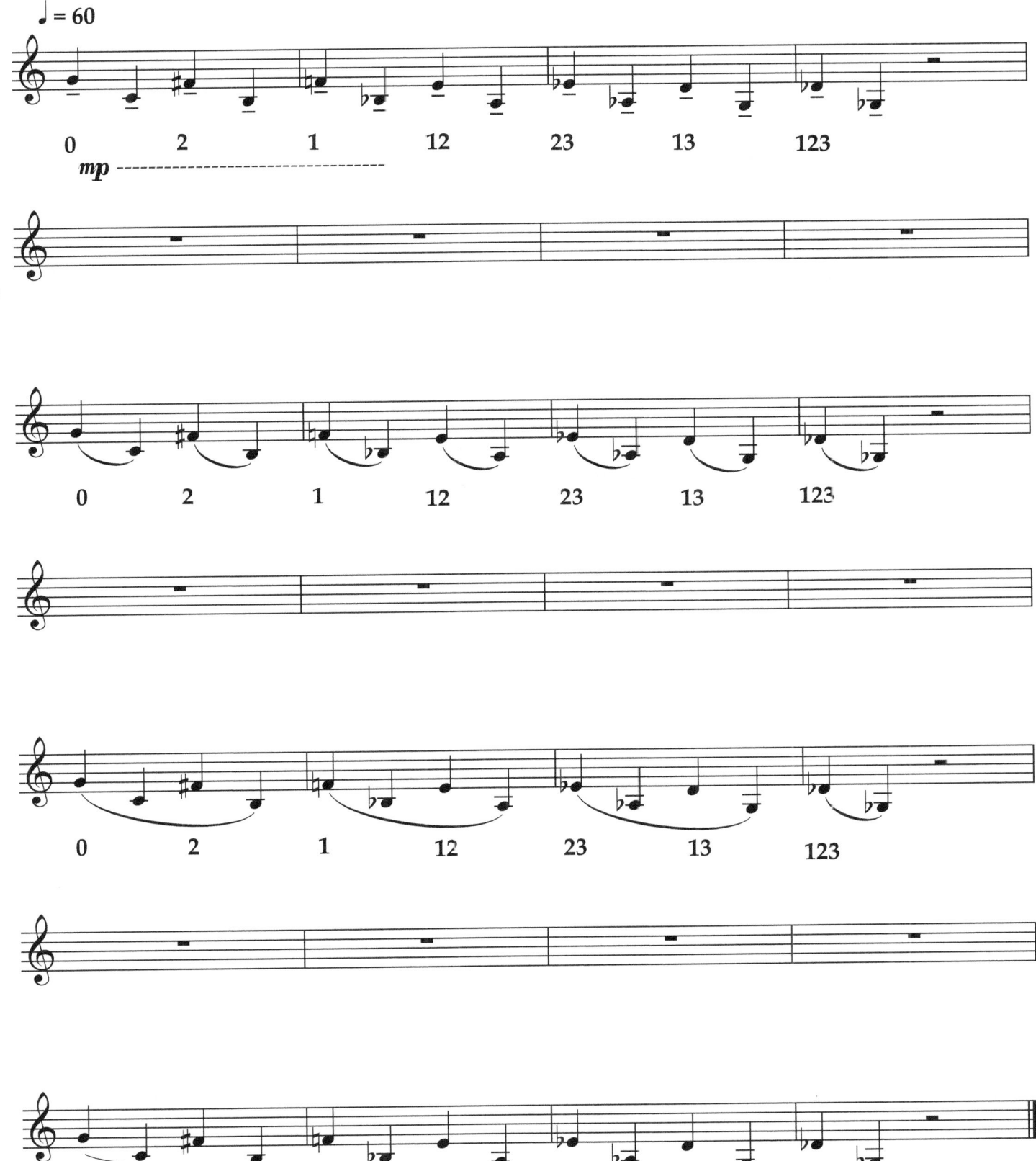

# Comments and Suggestions for Exercise 15 (faster)

Do not attempt this one until you are very good at playing exercise 15 at m.m. 60.

You must set the metronome to 80.

Obey the 4 consecutive measures of rests!

The entire exercise is medium soft - mp.

## Teacher or Student Notes:

# Exercise 15 (faster)

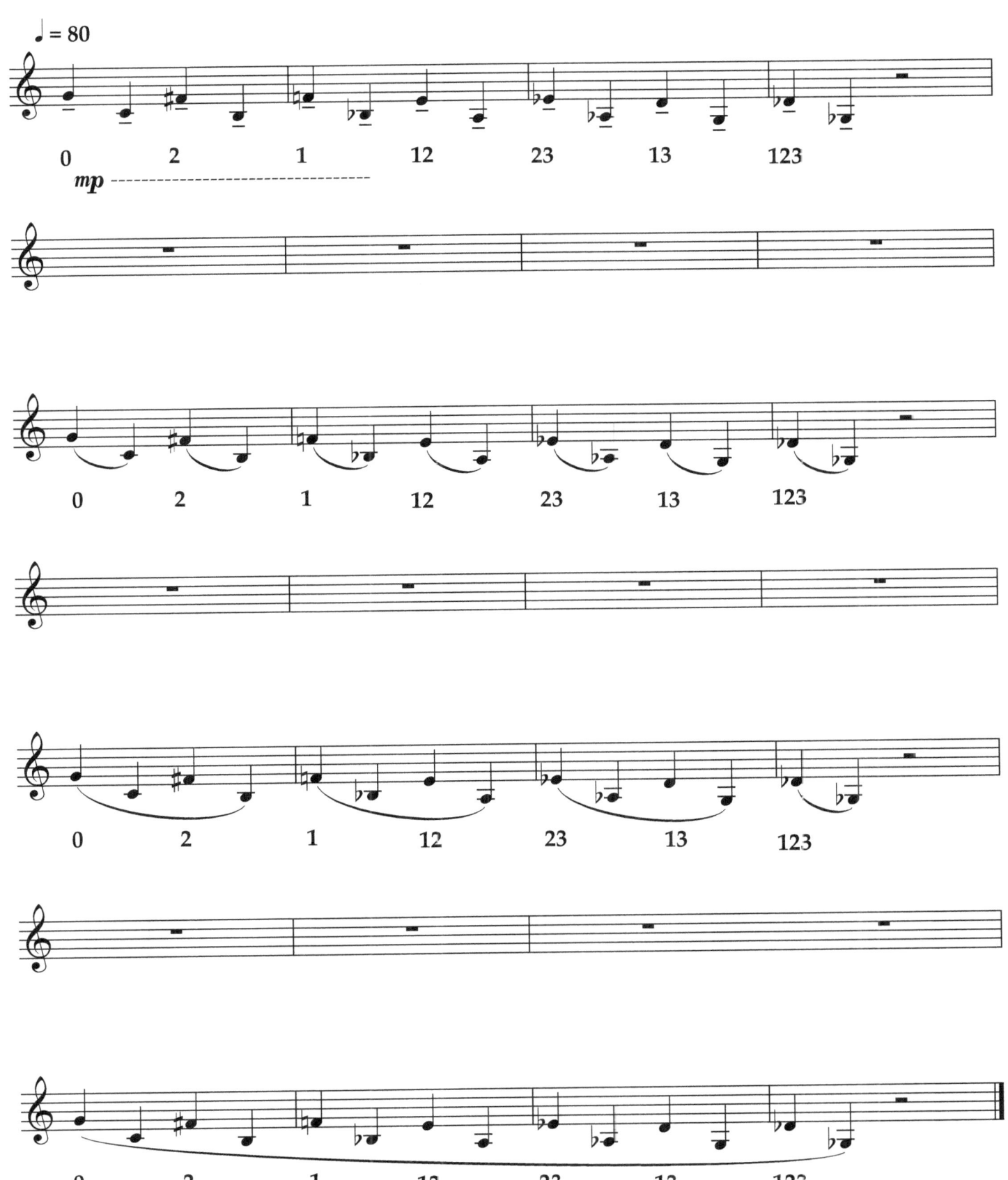

63

# Comments and Suggestions for Exercise 16

Carefully notice how the articulation changes from line to line.
Set the metronome and observe the 4 bar segments of rests.
The entire exercise is medium soft - mp.

## Teacher or Student Notes:

# Exercise 16

# Comments and Suggestions for Exercise 16 (faster)

You must set the metronome to 80 and observe the 4 bar segments of rests. The entire exercise is medium soft - mp.

## Teacher or Student Notes:

# Exercise 16 (faster)

67

# Comments and Suggestions for Exercise 17

We switch gears in Exercise 17. By now, you will have developed a certain "feel" or memorized placement of where notes are on the horn. Exercise 17 takes it to the next level by drilling over and over and dialing in exactly where these notes are by further developing this memorized feel.

The metronome is set at 72. Dynamics have moved up to medium loud - mf plus something new is being introduced: You will be fully taking the horn/mouthpiece off your mouth during each rest. Your goal is to be able to cleanly play each subsequent note engaging this "feel" of where the placement of the note should be. Strike the note cleanly each time without wobbling and without the dreaded "spiah" or chipped attack. Don't forget our "AH" to "EE" tongue arch strategy to cleanly move (slur) from a lower note to a higher note.

Teacher or Student Notes:

# Exercise 17

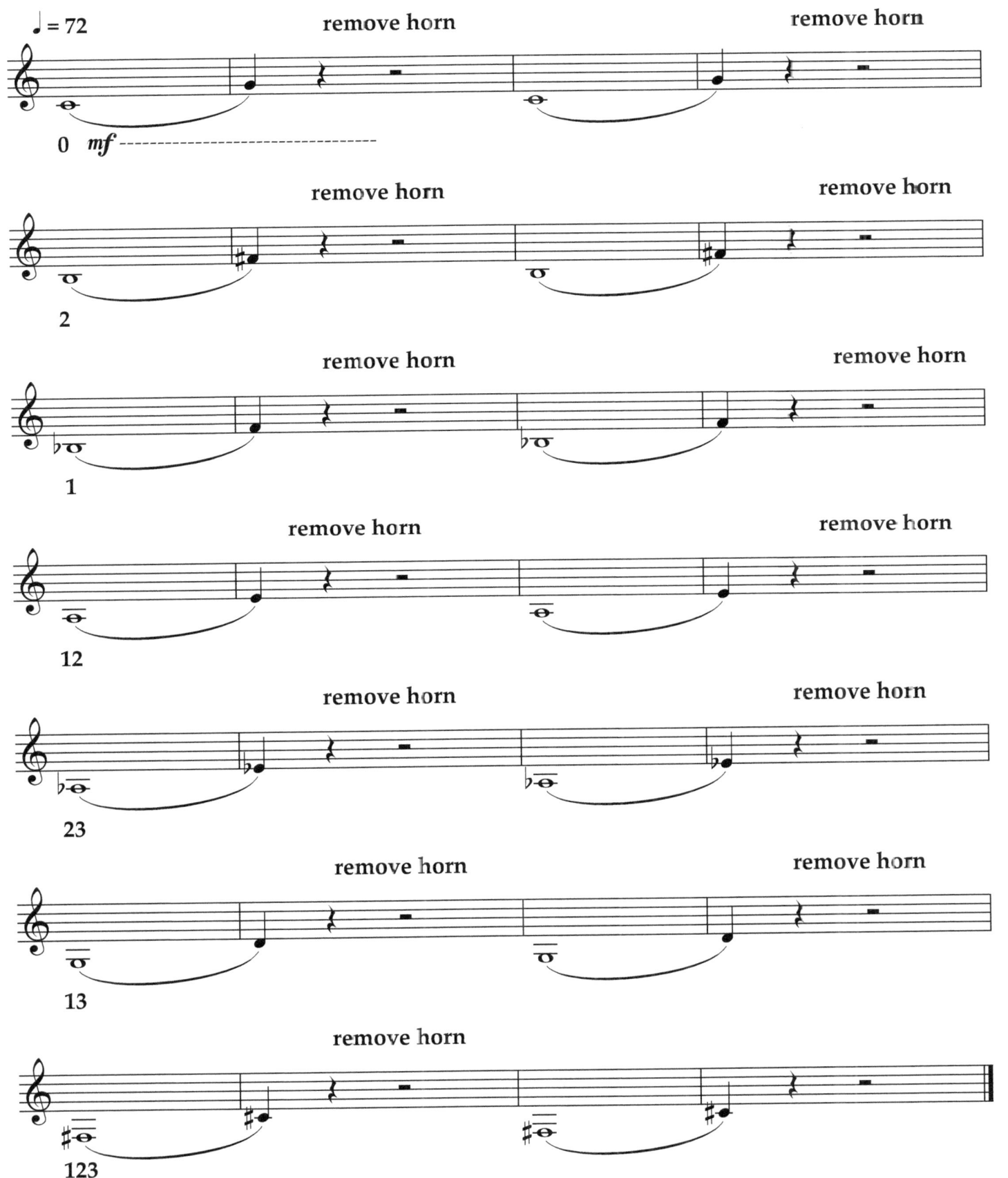

69

# Comments and Suggestions for Exercise 17 (faster)

Look out: You must set the metronome to 104. This is quite a bit faster than what you were just working on in Exercise 17.
The dynamic level is medium loud - mf.

## Teacher or Student Notes:

# Exercise 17 (faster)

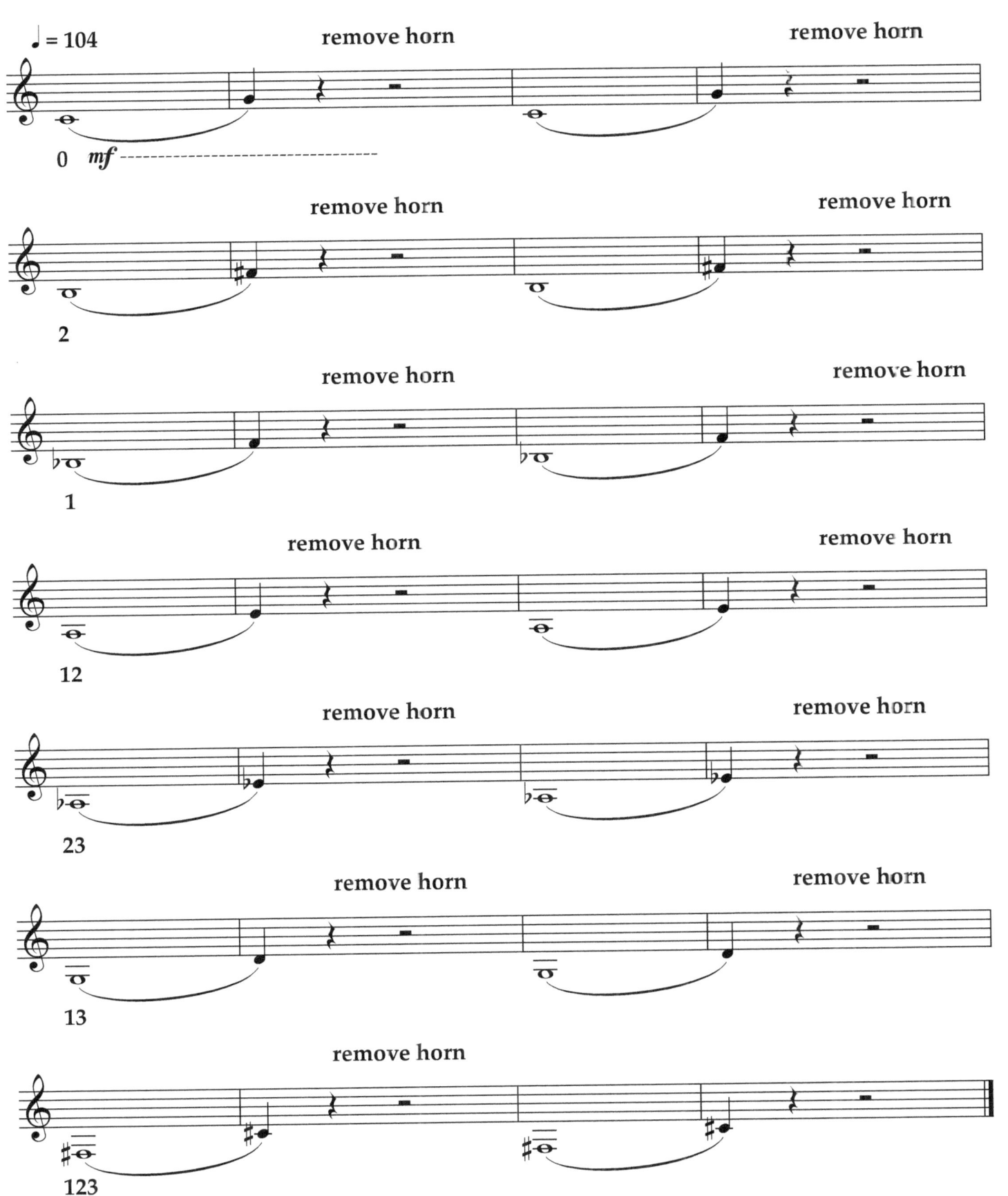

71

# Comments and Suggestions for Exercise 18

Exercise 18 is a continuation of working on "feel" and placement of notes.
Set the metronome.
The dynamic level is medium loud - mf.

## Teacher or Student Notes:

# Exercise 18

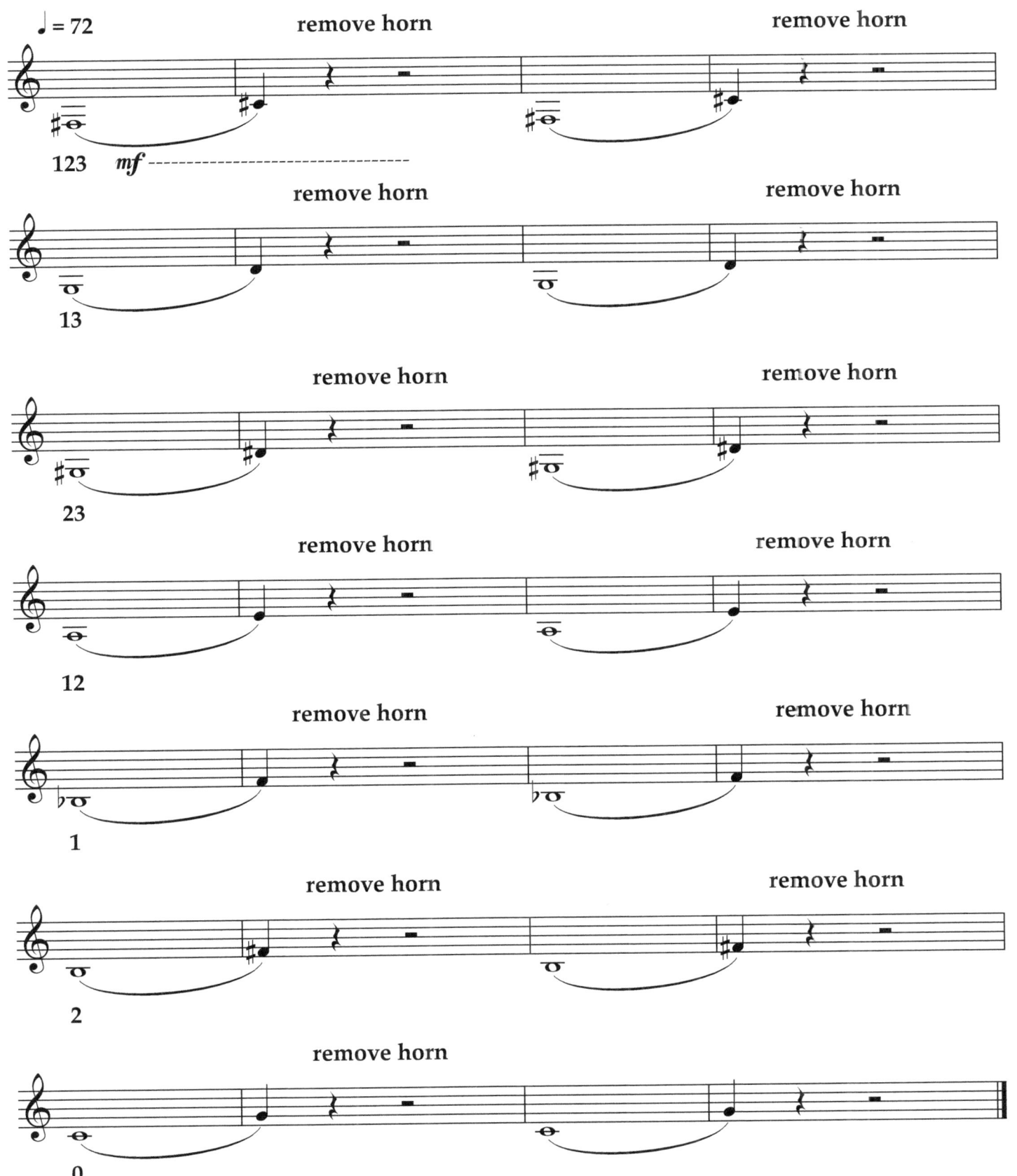

73

# Comments and Suggestions for Exercise 18 (faster)

You must set the metronome to 104.
The dynamic level is medium loud - mf.

## Teacher or Student Notes:

# Exercise 18 (faster)

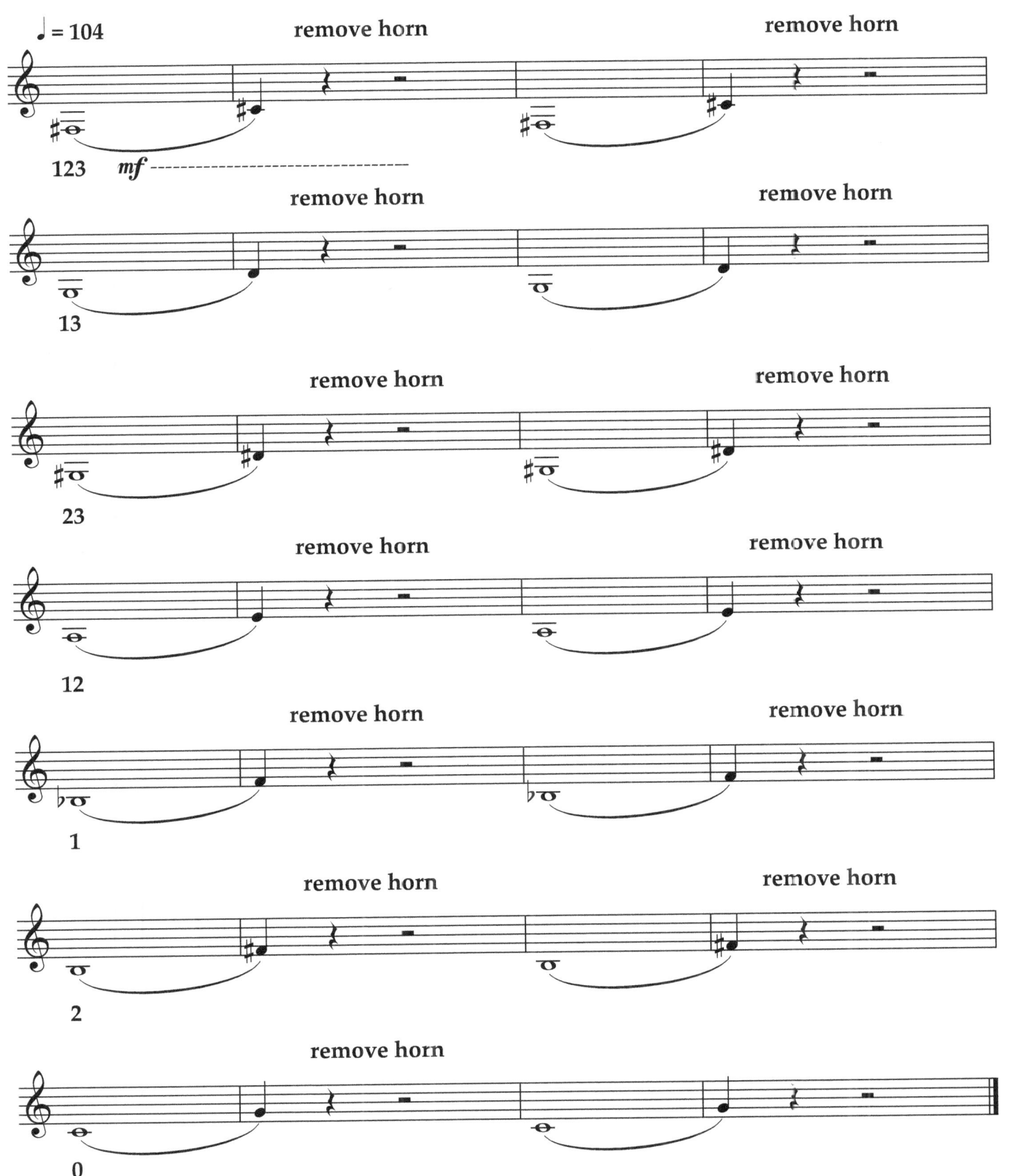

# Comments and Suggestions for Exercise 19 (slow)

You must set the metronome to 60. The dynamic level is medium soft - mp.

Exercise 19 comes in 4 flavors: Slow, Medium, Medium Fast, and Fast.

For many of you, the "fast" version might seem like an impossibility, but don't despair: Stay in your lane until you have mastered the speed of the one you are working on. Once you can smoothly and cleanly perform the slurs/trills, continue on to the next faster version. Don't be in a hurry. You are laying a rock solid foundation for your future self: The Advanced Trumpeter! We want that foundation to be of rock, not sand, which means you take your time until you get it right.

_Ultimate Goal:_ To be able to play each line in 1 breath (3 measures). If at first this seems impossible, attempt to play through the first 2 measures then take a breath before the ending whole note. At some point, you WILL be able to play the entire line for each valve combination: 123,13,23,12,1,2,0

Teacher or Student Notes:

# Exercise 19 (slow)

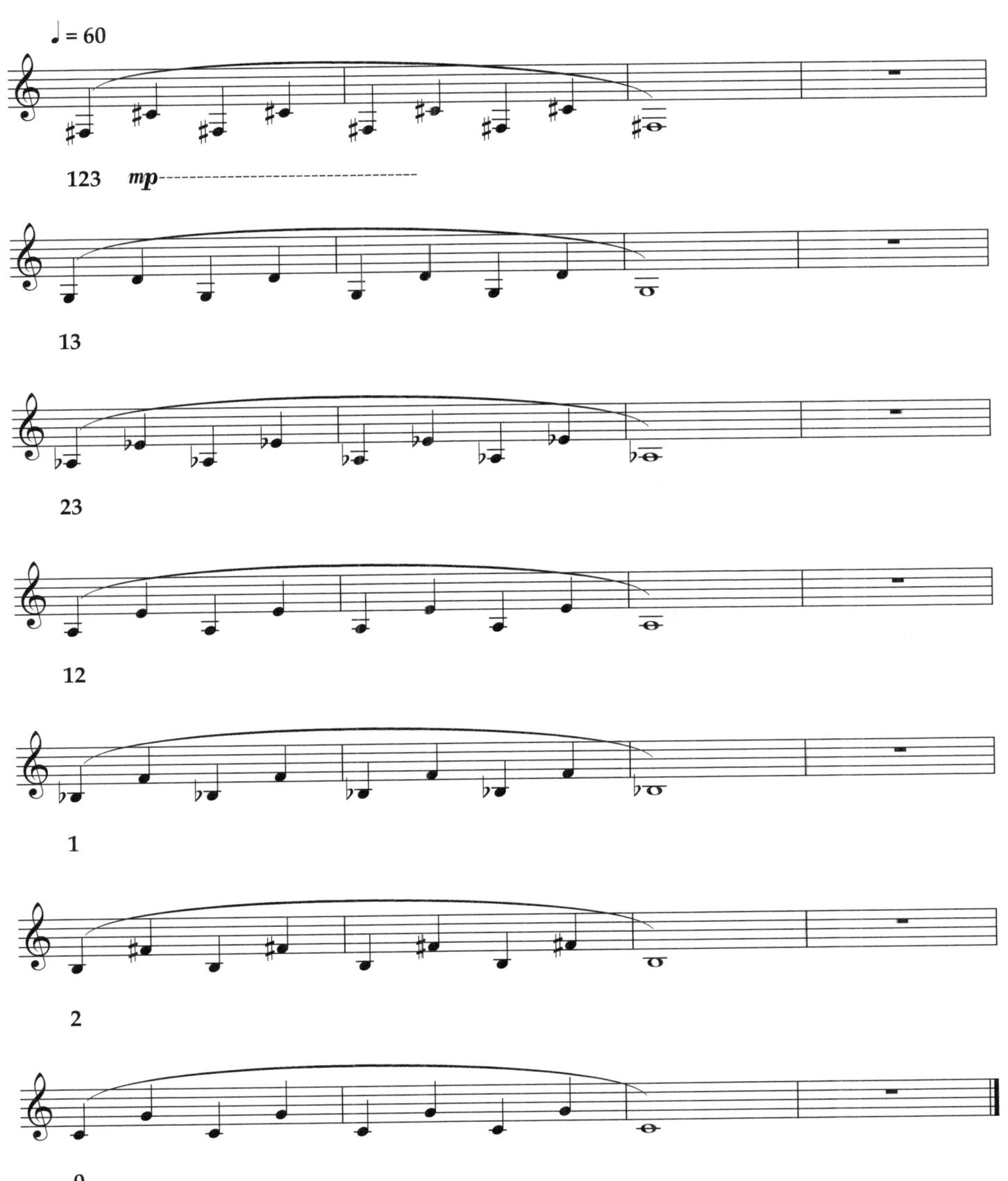

77

# Comments and Suggestions for Exercise 19 (medium)

You must set the metronome to 80. The dynamic level is medium soft - mp.
Exercise 19 comes in 4 flavors: Slow, Medium, Medium Fast, and Fast.

_Ultimate Goal:_ To be able to play each line in 1 breath (3 measures).
If at first this seems impossible, attempt to play through the first 2 measures then take a breath before the ending whole note. At some point, you WILL be able to play the entire line for each valve combination: 123,13,23,12,1,2,0

## Teacher or Student Notes:

# Exercise 19 (medium)

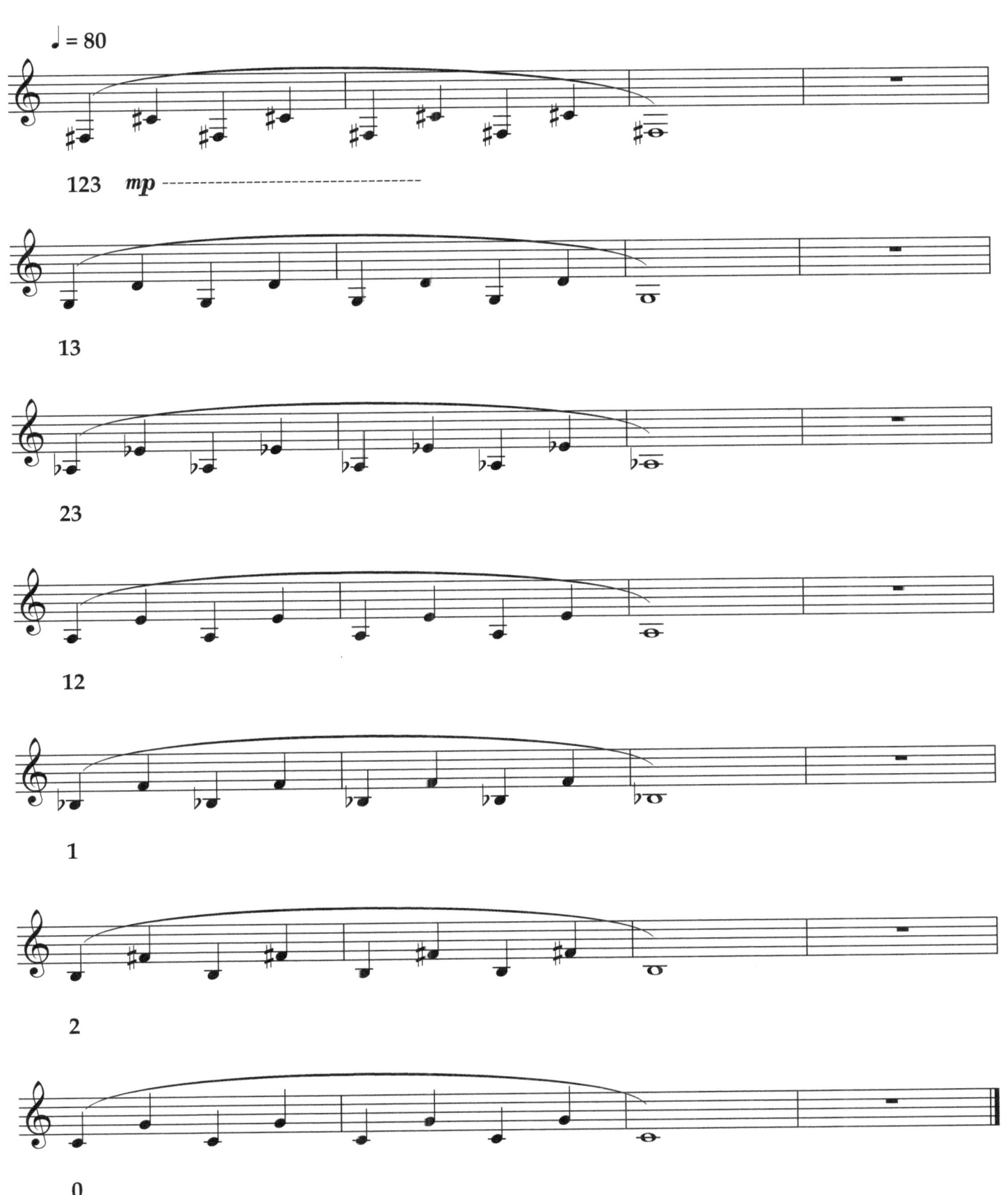

# Comments and Suggestions for Exercise 19 (medium fast)

You must set the metronome to 100. The dynamic level is medium soft - mp. Exercise 19 comes in 4 flavors: Slow, Medium, Medium Fast, and Fast.

*Ultimate Goal:* To be able to play each line in 1 breath (3 measures).
If at first this seems impossible, attempt to play through the first 2 measures then take a breath before the ending whole note. At some point, you WILL be able to play the entire line for each valve combination: 123,13,23,12,1,2,0

## Teacher or Student Notes:

# Exercise 19 (medium fast)

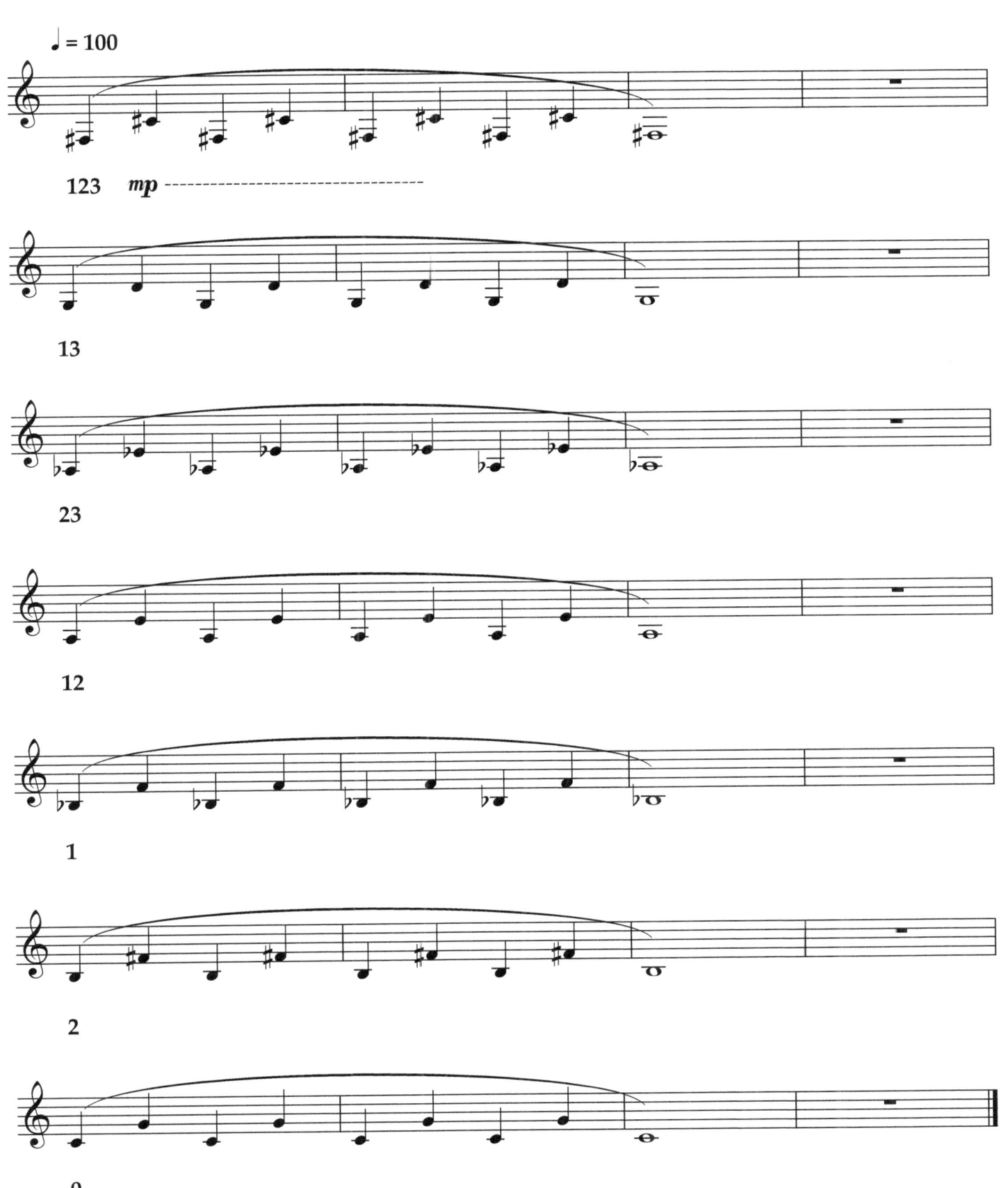

81

# Comments and Suggestions for Exercise 19 (fast)

You must set the metronome to 120. The dynamic level is medium soft - mp.
If you are now working on this version...
CONGRATULATIONS! Great Accomplishment!


## Teacher or Student Notes:

# Exercise 19 (fast)

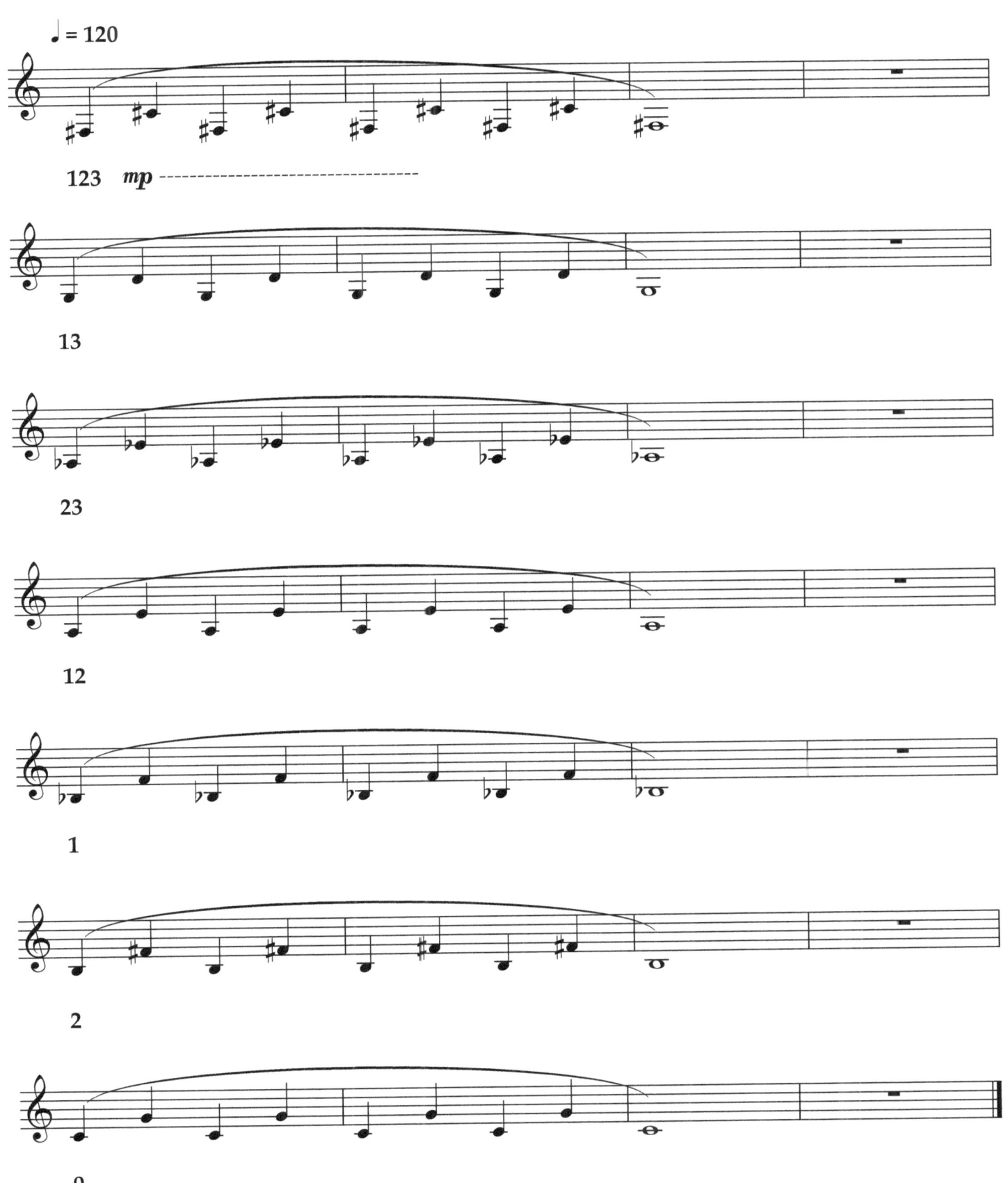

83

# Comments and Suggestions for Exercise 20 (slow)

You must set the metronome to 60. The dynamic level is medium soft - mp. Exercise 20 comes in 4 speeds just like Exercise 19. You know the drill so no need to repeat what was said in Exercise 19. You will work diligently until the speed is accomplished, then move on to the next faster version.

## Teacher or Student Notes:

# Exercise 20 (slow)

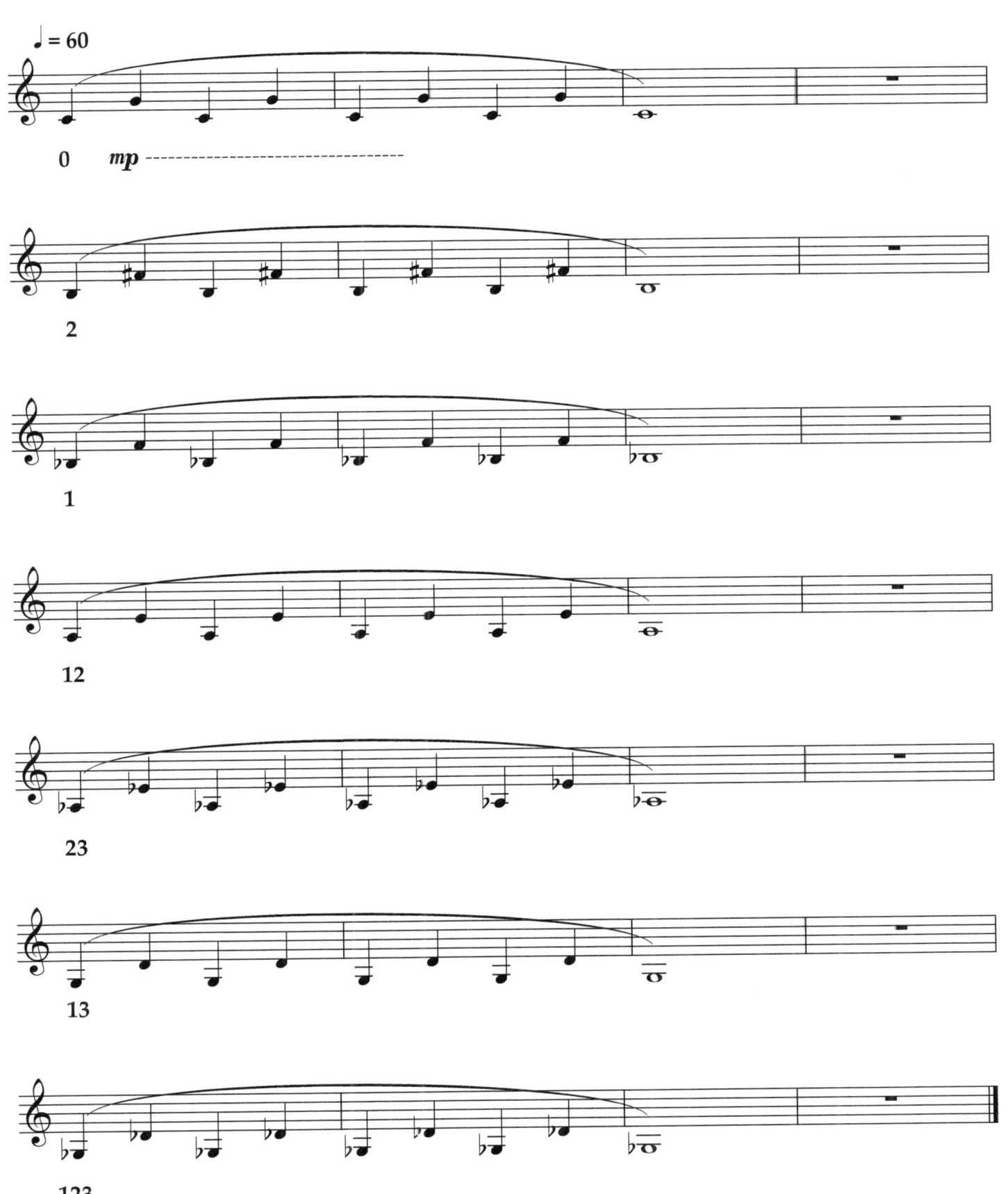

# Comments and Suggestions for Exercise 20 (medium)

You must set the metronome to 80.
The dynamic level is medium soft - mp.

## Teacher or Student Notes:

# Exercise 20 (medium)

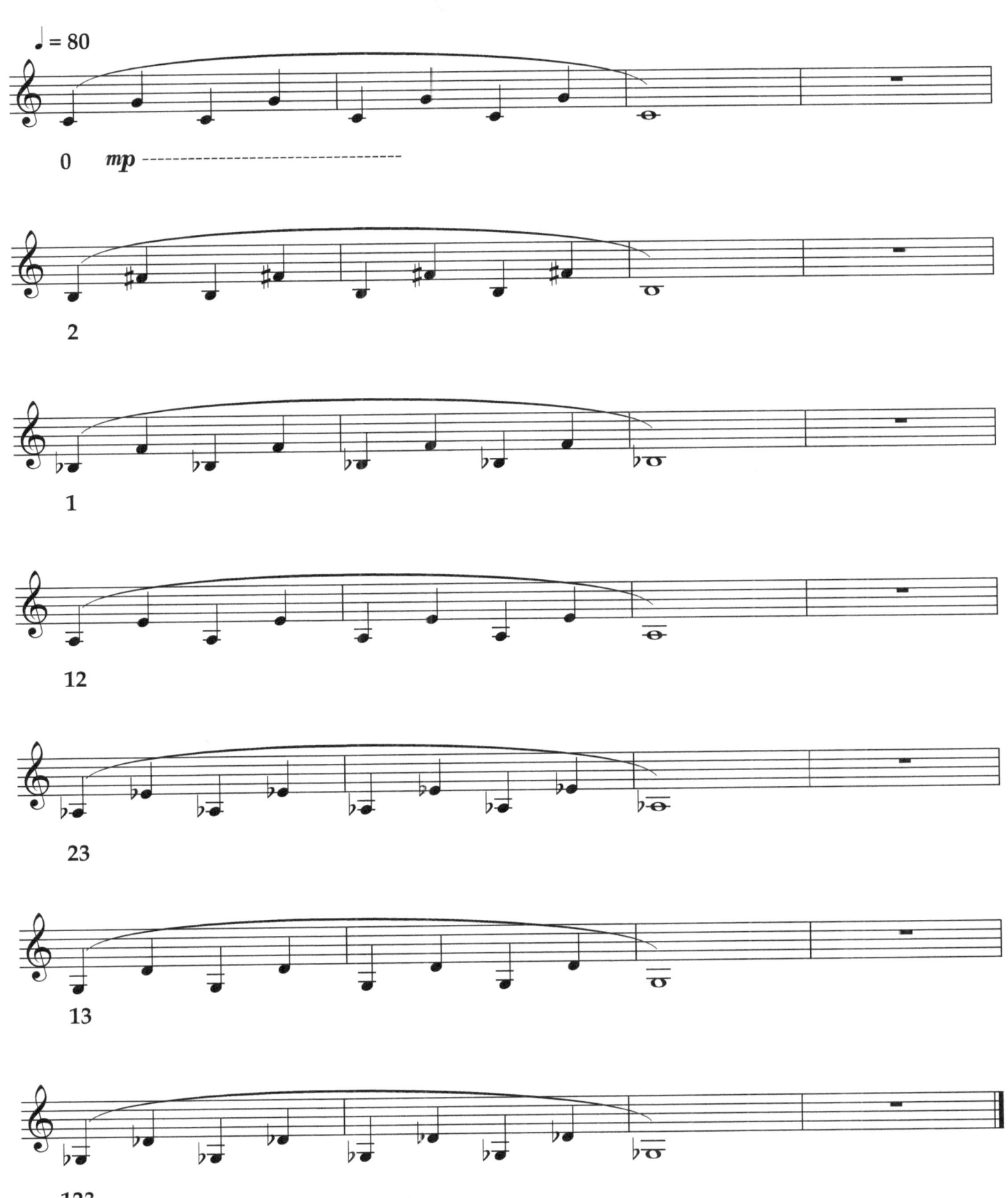

# Comments and Suggestions for Exercise 20 (medium fast)

You must set the metronome to 100.
The dynamic level is medium soft - mp.

## Teacher or Student Notes:

# Exercise 20 (medium fast)

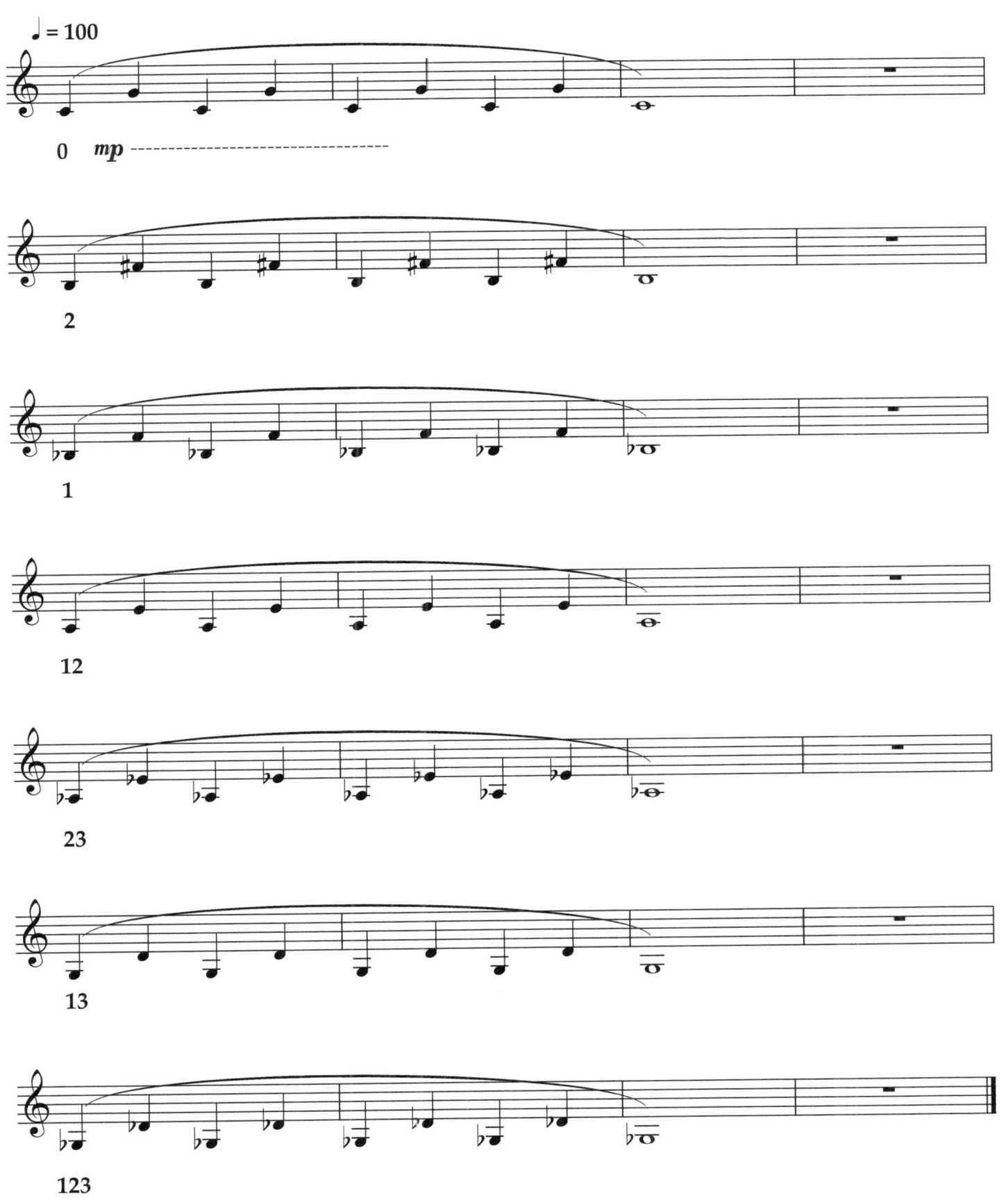

89

# Comments and Suggestions for Exercise 20 (fast)

You must set the metronome to 120.

The dynamic level is medium soft - mp.

If you made it to this version, Congratulations!

Pat yourself on the back because this is a great accomplishment!

## Teacher or Student Notes:

# Exercise 20 (fast)

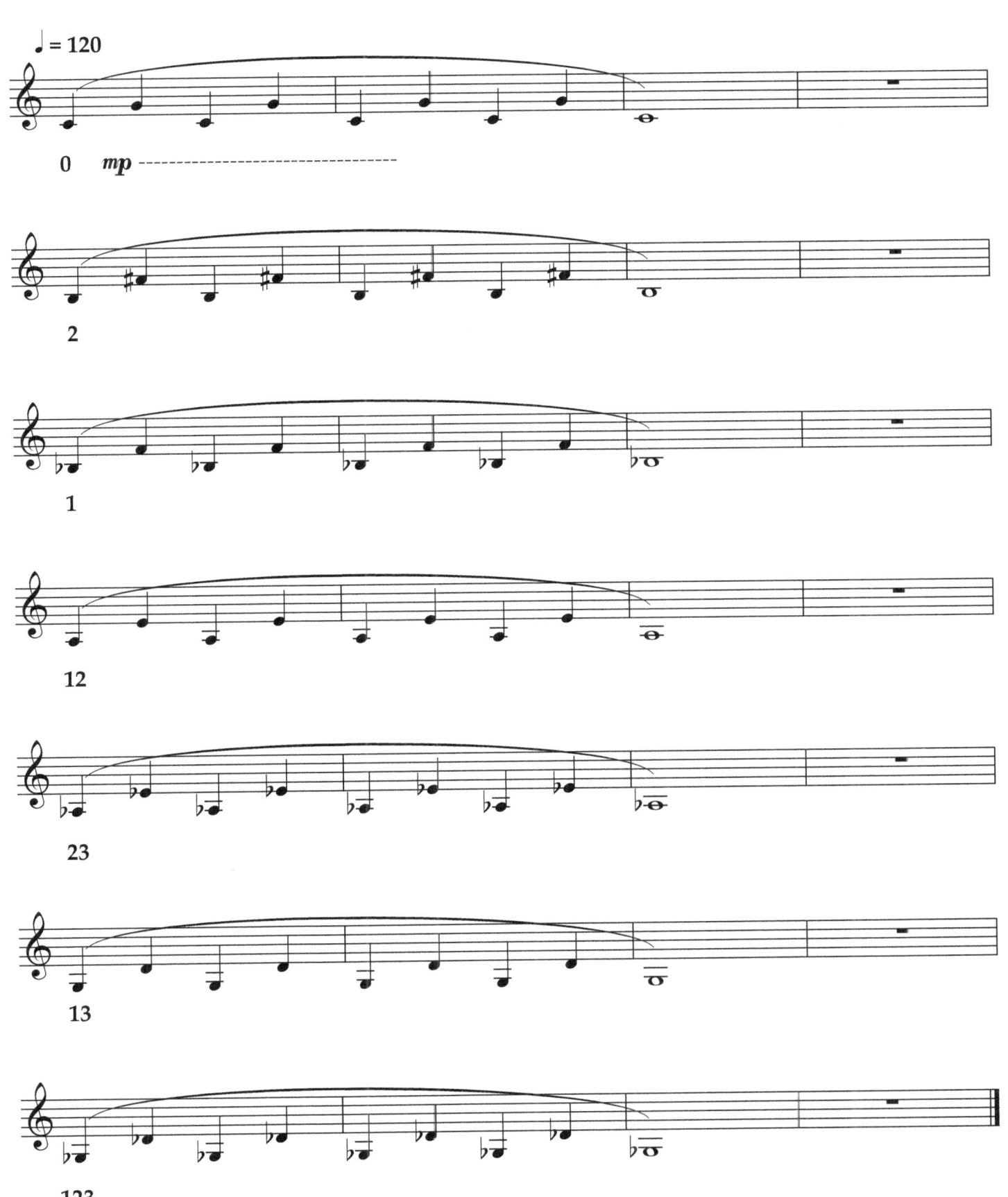

# Comments and Suggestions for Exercise 21

You must set the metronome to 72. The dynamic level is medium soft - mp.

With Exercise 21, we are increasing the difficulty. Most of the previous exercises in this book have been a back and forth between 2 notes. Now, we will be slurring up and down with 3 notes! This is like adding weight to a barbell in the gym. Be patient. Previously, you worked up to a good speed in Exercise 19 and 20, but that speed may appear to come down temporarily due to adding a third note.

Obey the two measures of rest at the end of each line.

## Teacher or Student Notes:

# Exercise 21

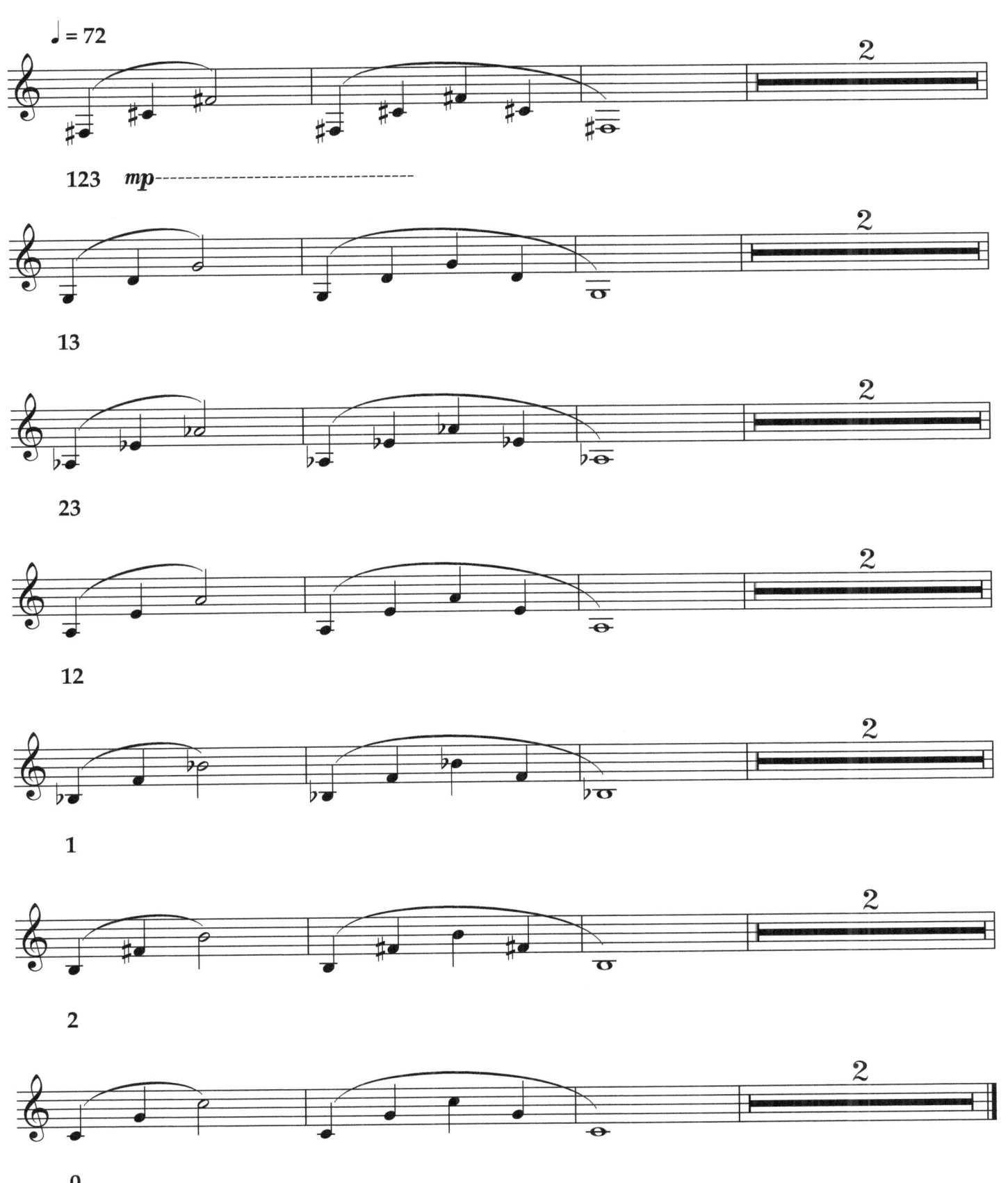

# Comments and Suggestions for Exercise 21 (faster)

You must set the metronome to 100. The dynamic level is medium soft - mp.
The first version of Exercise 21 gave you a chance to get used to slurring 3 notes at a slower speed. This version moves along very quickly.
Obey the two measures of rest at the end of each line.

## Teacher or Student Notes:

# Exercise 21 (faster)

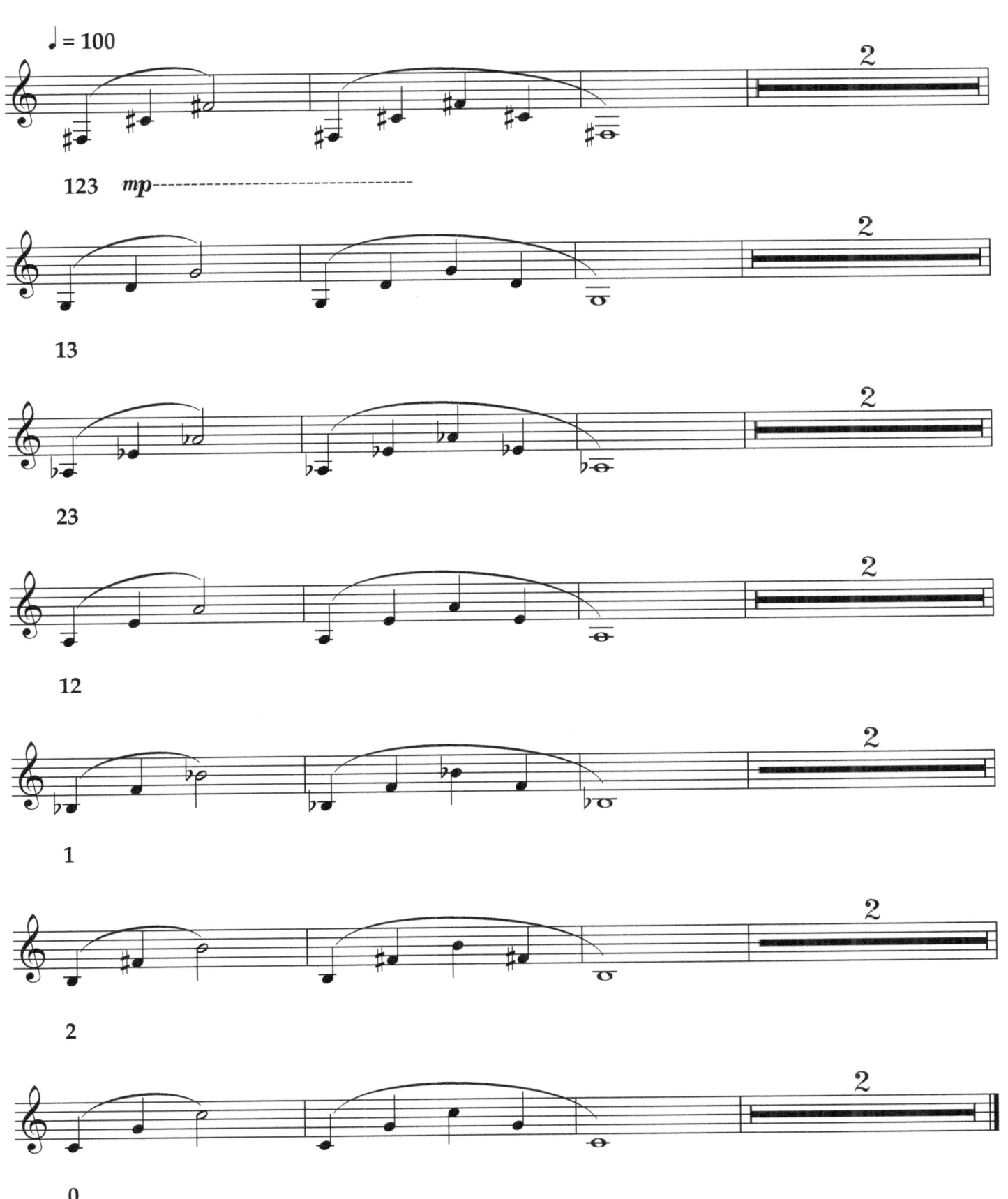

# Comments and Suggestions for Exercise 22

You must set the metronome to 72.

The dynamic level is medium soft - mp.

Obey the 2 measure rest at the end of each line.

## Teacher or Student Notes:

# Exercise 22

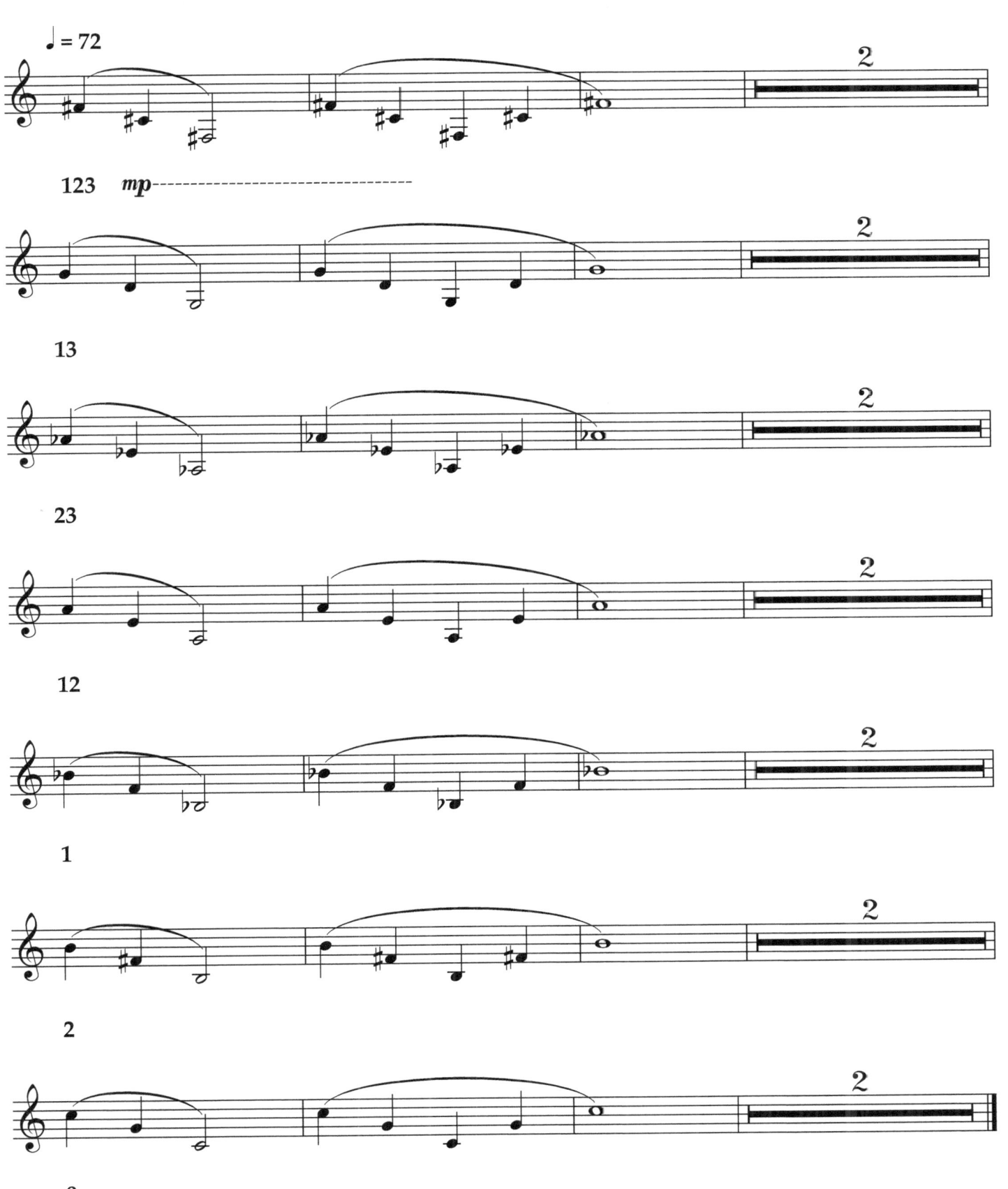

# Comments and Suggestions for Exercise 22 (faster)

You must set the metronome to 100.

The dynamic level is medium soft - mp.

Obey the 2 measure rest at the end of each line.


Teacher or Student Notes:

# Exercise 22 (faster)

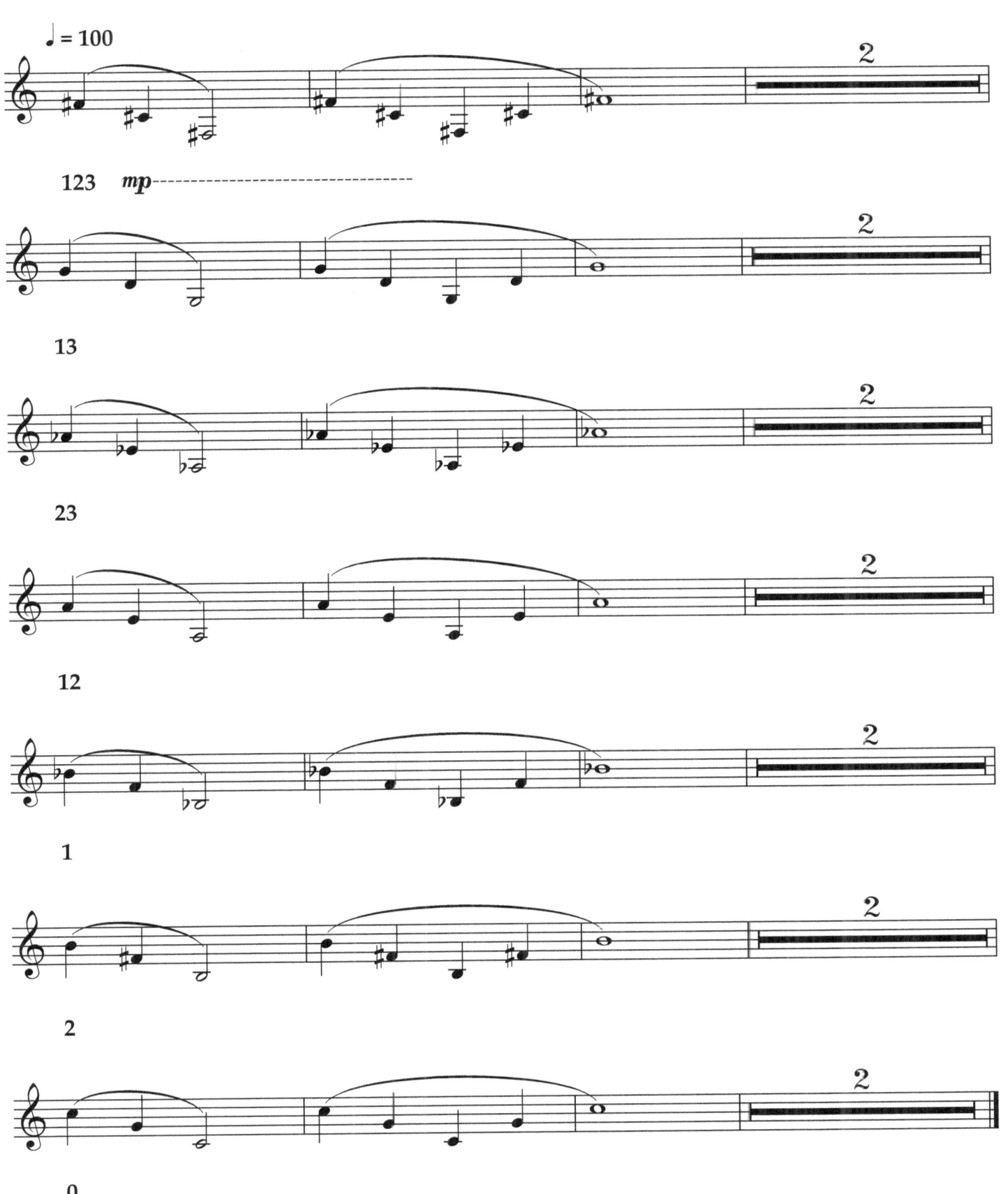

99

# Comments and Suggestions for Exercise 23

You must set the metronome to 60. The dynamic level is medium loud - mf.

With Exercise 23 we are switching gears. We will be slurring, but not lip slurring.

Play these notes using regular fingerings. This means we will be able to use our valves to move between notes. You will notice that on certain notes, FLEXIBILITY is required. For example: The very first measure has you slurring between G and A. Think that's easy? It's not, especially as you go faster. On the 3rd line you will be slurring from Low C to D. You will definitely notice that flexibility is required. To a lesser extent, you will also feel the flexibility demand as you play the very Low G to Low A. The other notes in this exercise seem to pop right out without too much effort or flexibility concerns.

## Teacher or Student Notes:

# Exercise 23

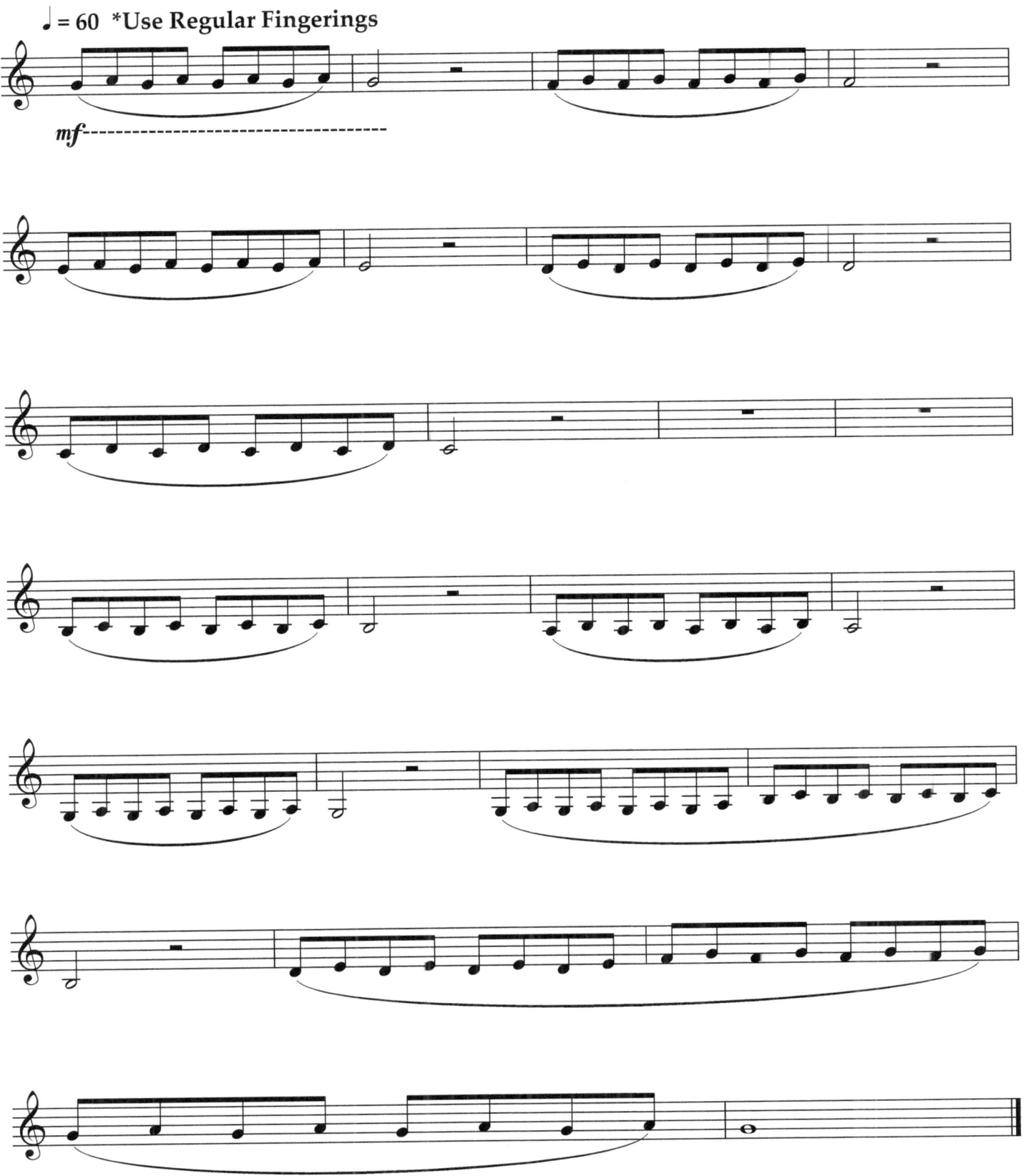

# Comments and Suggestions for Exercise 24

You won't need the metronome. The dynamic level is extremely soft - ppp.

Exercise 24 is an exercise in lip buzzing. For many of you, this is brand new. That's fine. This is called free lip buzzing or simply lip buzzing. When we lip buzz, we don't use the horn or the mouthpiece to make a sound. We are actually buzzing just the lips to produce the pitch (the sound).

The first half of the exercise has you playing a 2nd line G on your horn. You are doing this to get the pitch. You play G on your trumpet then take it off your lips. You then BUZZ your lips together (no trumpet) attempting to produce the G you previously just played on your instrument. It may take you a few tries, but that's ok. Please notice you are buzzing an octave lower than what you played on your horn. You are buzzing a low G to begin with.

I have found most beginning students and comeback players can buzz this note. If you cannot, don't be discouraged. Move on down to the second half of this exercise because the 2nd note for buzzing drops down to F (which may be easier).

Buzz as softly as you can to get the sound. Obey all rests, especially the big, long 4 measure rest in the middle.

## Teacher or Student Notes:

# Exercise 24

Freely - very, very soft buzzing

Play      *ppp*    Buzz!    Play      *ppp*    Buzz!

Play      *ppp*    Buzz!    Play      *ppp*    Buzz!

Play      *ppp*    Buzz!    Play      *ppp*    Buzz!

4

Play      *ppp*    Buzz!    Play      *ppp*    Buzz!

Play      *ppp*    Buzz!    Play      *ppp*    Buzz!

Play      *ppp*    Buzz!    Play      *ppp*    Buzz!

# Comments and Suggestions for Exercise 25

You won't need the metronome for the playing part. However, when you count the 4 measures of rests after each buzz, use 60 on the metronome. This will ensure your lips are rested before continuing. The dynamic level is soft - p.

Exercise 25 is an exercise in Mouthpiece Buzzing. For many of you, this is brand new. That's fine. It is easier than the previous lip buzzing exercise found in Exercise 24. Yes, you will only be playing on the mouthpiece - no horn! You can use your horn to hear the correct starting pitch. For example, at the beginning you see a middle C sliding or "glissing" (glissando) down to a low C. First, play that C on your trumpet. Keep that pitch in your head or hum it while taking the mouthpiece out of the horn. Play that same note, but only on your mouthpiece. Play it soft and let it slide smoothly down the octave to low C. Hold the low C for as long as possible until you run out of air. Using 60 on the metronome, begin counting those 4 measures of rests. After the 4 measures of rests, repeat the above procedure for the remainder of the exercise. Obey all 4 measure groups of rests. If the 4 measures of rests are not enough, it is fine if you want to double it to 8 measures. No matter what, do not skip the rests!

## Teacher or Student Notes:

# Exercise 25

**Mouthpiece only - no horn**

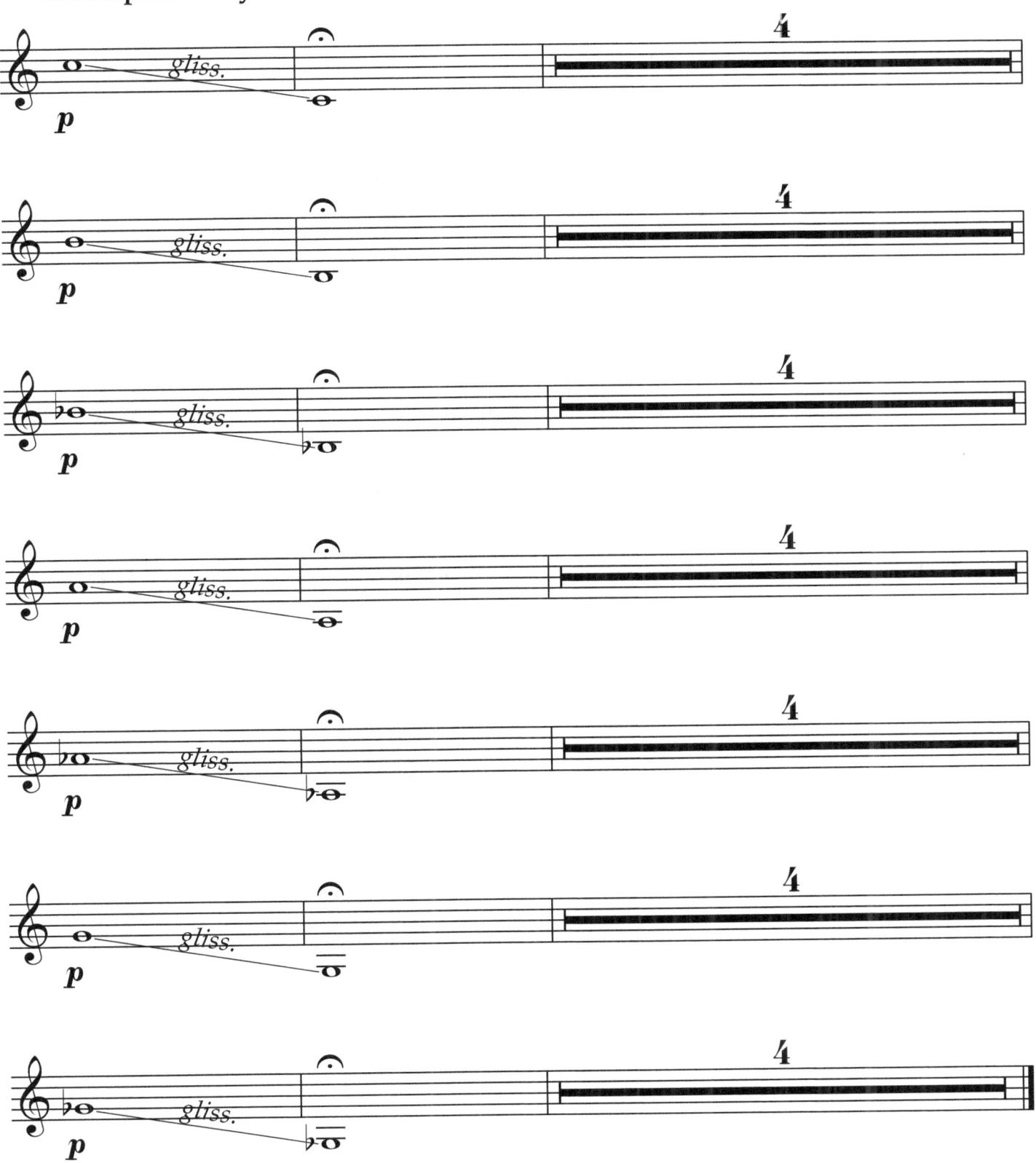

# Comments and Suggestions for Exercise 26

You won't need the metronome for the playing part. However, when you count the 4 measures of rests after each buzz, use 60 on the metronome. This will ensure your lips are rested before continuing. The dynamic level is soft - p.

Exercise 26 is an exercise in Mouthpiece Buzzing. The directions are the same as the Mouthpiece Buzzing you just did in Exercise 25, but with one added concern: TONGUE ARCH. You will need to use "AH" to "EE". It will be harder to glissando up an octave on your mouthpiece as compared to simply sliding down the octave. Again, follow the same instructions from Exercise 25. Hold the fermata note for as long as you can. Using 60 on the metronome, begin counting those 4 measures of rests. After the 4 measures of rests, repeat the above procedure for the remainder of the exercise. Obey all 4 measure groups of rests. If the 4 measures of rests are not enough, it is fine if you want to double it to 8 measures. No matter what, do not skip the rests!

## Teacher or Student Notes:

# Exercise 26

**Mouthpiece only - no horn**

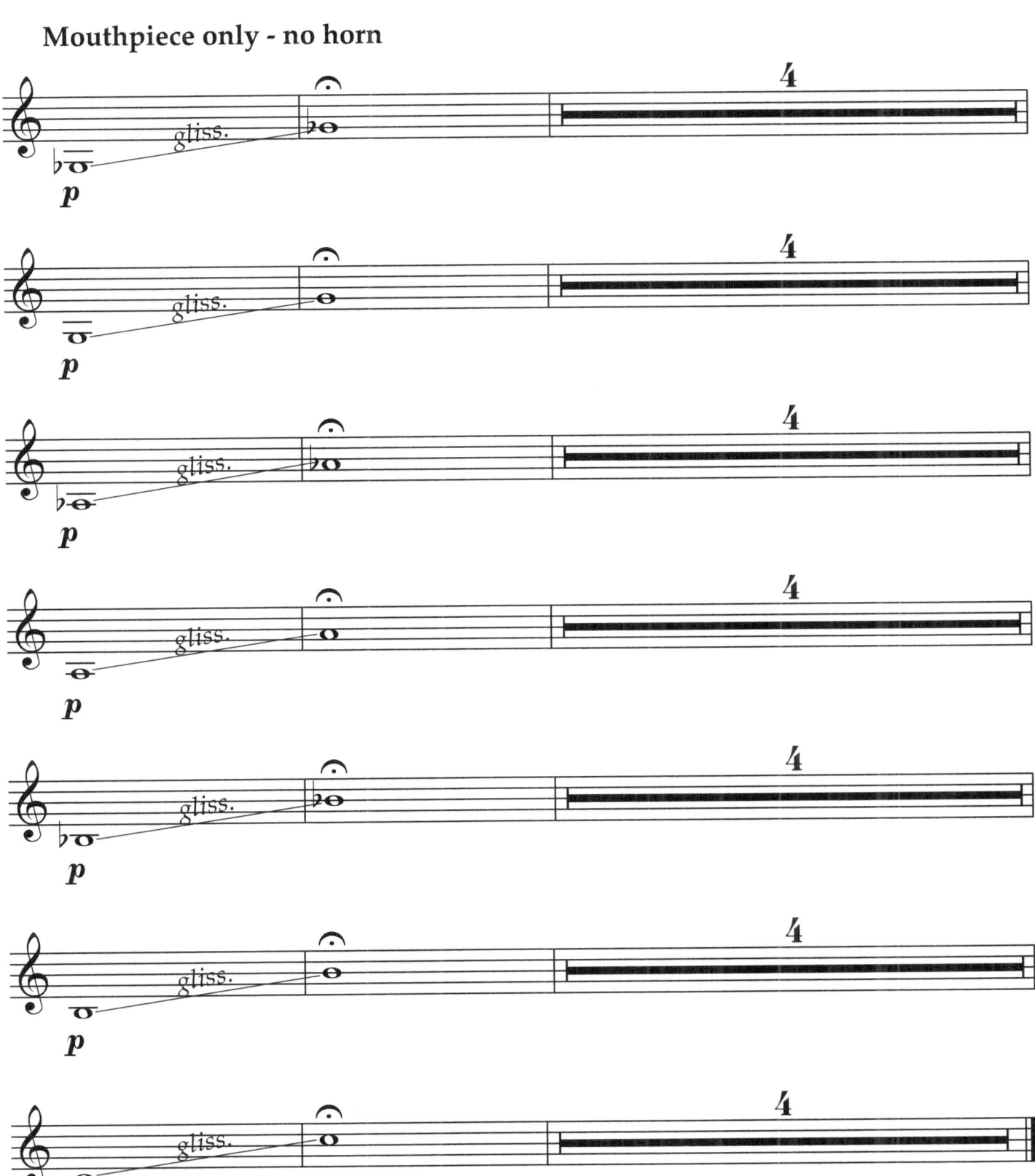

# Comments and Suggestions for Exercise 27

If by now, you really hadn't figured out the Tongue Arch Technique, here's your chance. The tongue plays an important part when it comes to trumpet playing...almost as much as the lips! The speed and rests are not written in stone as the playing exercises in this book. Do try starting at 80 on the metronome. If you feel like you would prefer faster, go for it! After a few days of practicing these tongue arch exercises, if you are feeling good and your tongue is not hurting, you
may repeat Exercise 27 for a double dose!

## Teacher or Student Notes:

# Exercise 27

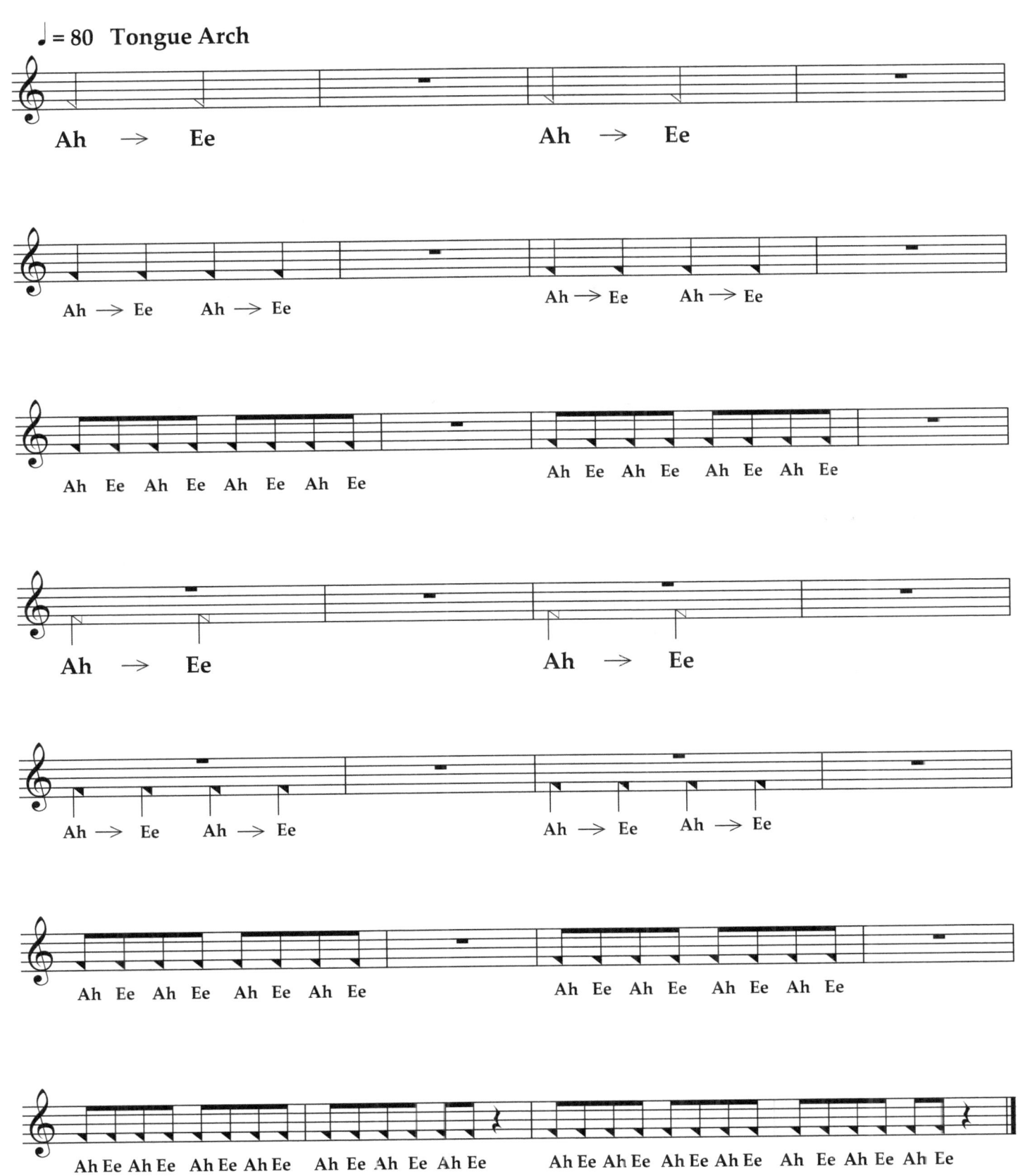

# Comments and Suggestions for Exercise 28

You are not playing these on your trumpet. You are "saying" these. Another tongue exercise. This one targets the very back of your tongue by using the syllable, "KA". Remember: A stronger, more coordinated tongue, means a trumpet player who is having an easier time playing the horn! Set your metronome to 80. Obey the rests.

You are vocalizing the K sound through "KA". The dynamic level is very loud - ff. However, you don't need to scream. The force and the attack is what needs to be loud. You could also substitute the word "LOUD" for "PERCUSSIVE", or "FORCEFUL". So, I suppose LOUD -FF could be misleading.

I can perform these by almost whispering yet achieve a very harsh type effect. I do not advise performing these in front of a friend...unless they have a towel! You want to deliver a very harsh "KA" sound very similar to karate students testing for a new belt. While performing their Kata's, you will hear them shout: "KIAH". We are doing something similar here, but removing the "iah" part because that softens it. A pure "KA" is very percussive and harsh compared to "kiah".


## Teacher or Student Notes:

# Exercise 28

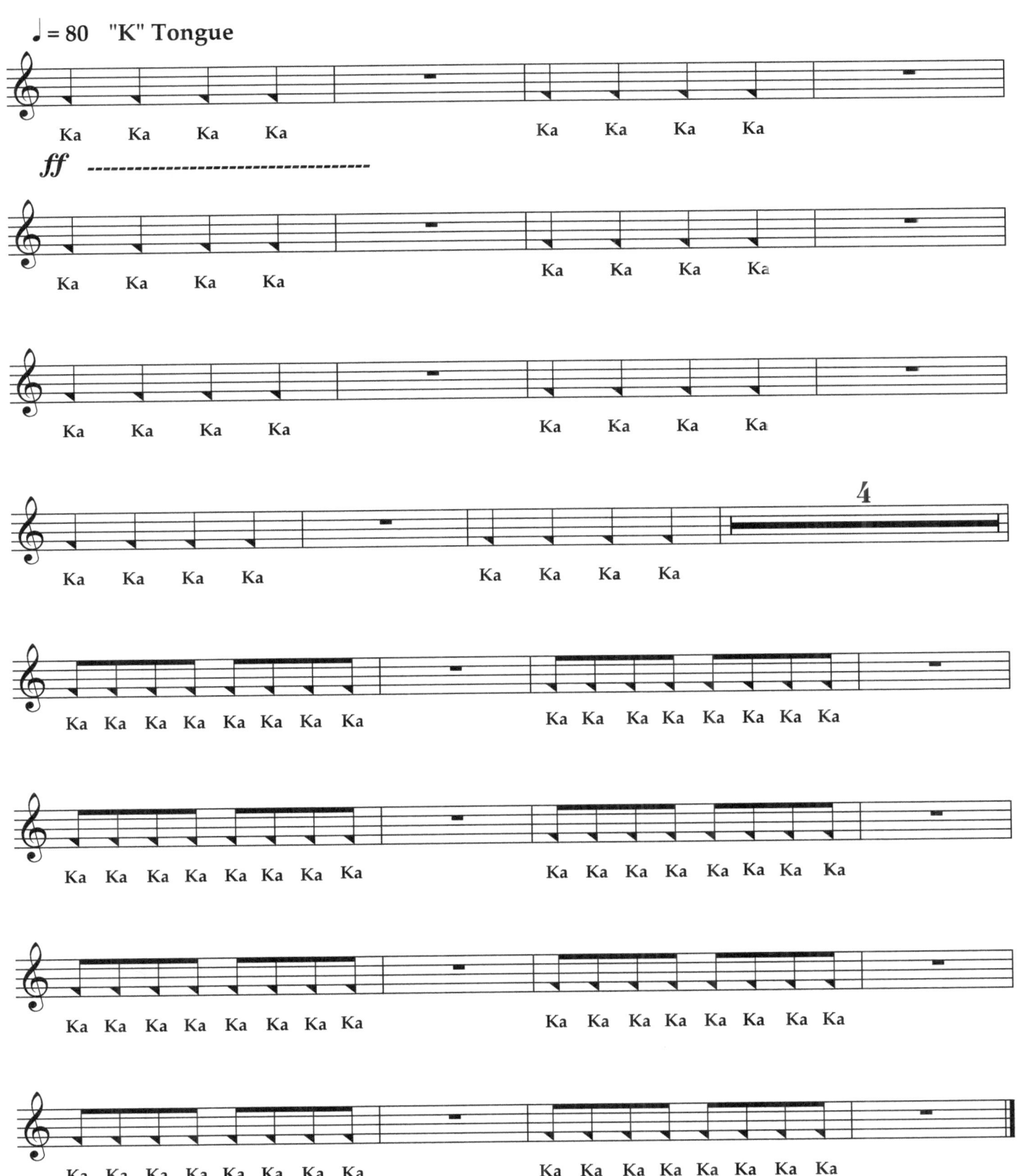

# Comments and Suggestions for Exercise 29

I consider Exercise 29 and Exercise 30 as the two final exams or cumulative studies of the book. I suppose you could also use the word Etude. You will use your regular trumpet valve fingerings and play these like you would in band class or in a piece of music. Set the metronome to 80. Play medium soft - mp. You are going for a smooth, seamless drop into each note of the descending arpeggio. Make these very, very smooth! Take a very big breath before you begin because you will be holding out the lowest note until you run out of air. Use the 3 rests to not only rest, but also catch your breath. If you have breathing or lung issues and need to double these rests, not a problem. However, do not short change the written 3 measures of rests. You must rest at least 3 measures between each playing section.

## Teacher or Student Notes:

# Exercise 29

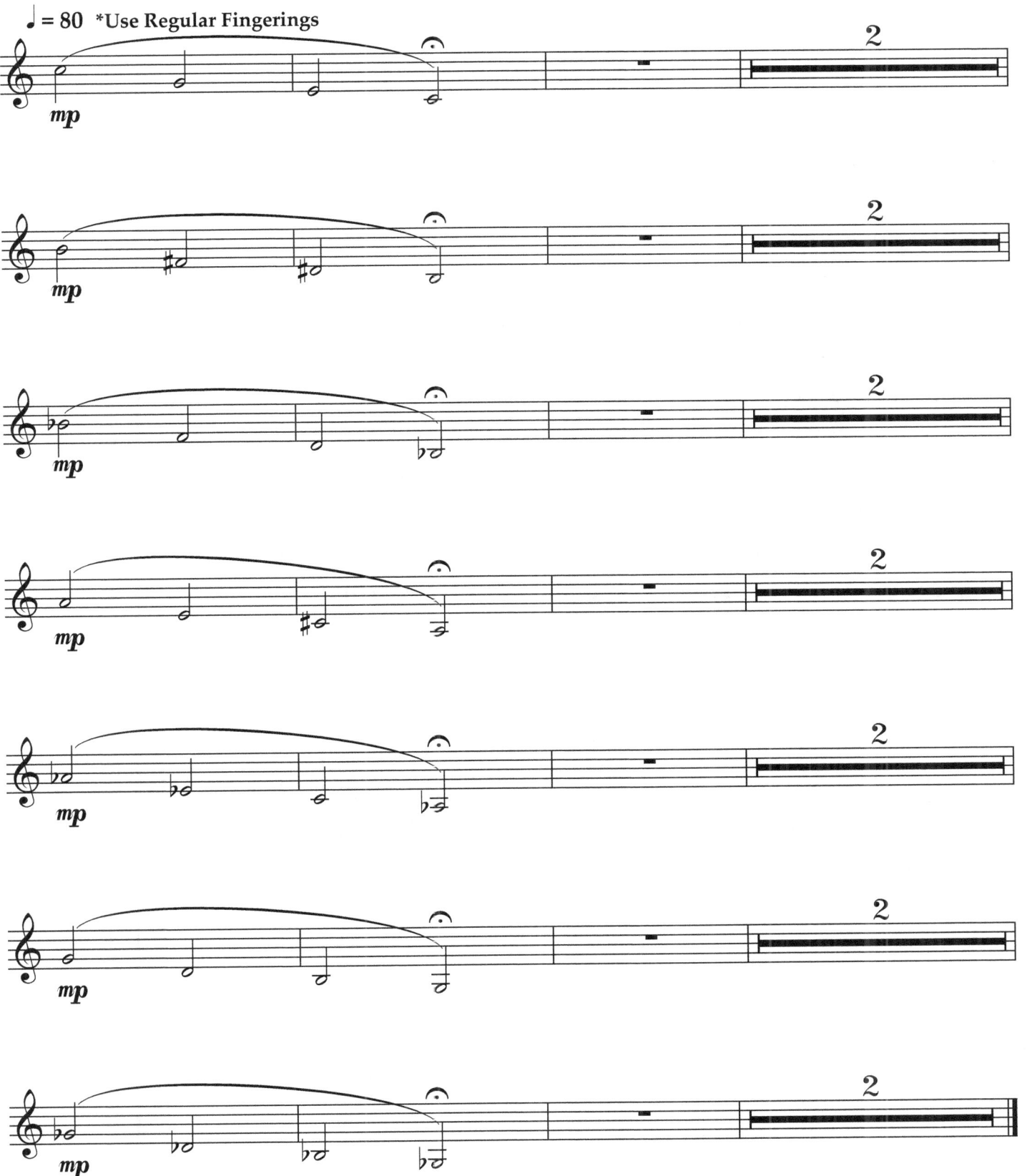

# Comments and Suggestions for Exercise 30

As I mentioned in Exercise 29, I consider Exercise 29 and Exercise 30 as the two final exams or cumulative studies of the book. You will use your regular trumpet valve fingerings and play these like you would in band class or in a piece of music. Set the metronome to 60.

NOTICE: These notes are tongued! Play the notes leading up to the fermata medium soft - mp. When you arrive at the fermata, you will see the mf under it. You will play the note under the fermata medium loud. You will also see an accent. I want you to be aggressive on these notes. An accent means you have to use more tongue and more air. When you accent a note, you are "bringing out" or emphasizing that particular note. You can decide to hold each fermata note until you run out of air or if not, you may simply hold the fermata equal to 2 or 3 whole notes. Notice the eighth rest that precedes each fermata whole note. You may freely take the rest out of tempo so that you can completely fill up your lungs with a fresh supply of air. This is your chance to take a big breath so that you can smack that note (accent it) and play it medium loud plus hold it for a good, long time.

The last 2 lines of Exercise 30 will truly be your ultimate test because we have not yet played higher than middle C in the staff. If you have diligently practiced this book through all the exercises like I prescribed, I have full faith and confidence that you either will be able to hit (play) both the D and the High G at the end of Exercise 30, or you will come mighty close to doing it.

## Teacher or Student Notes:

# Exercise 30

# Now What?

First of all, let me say: Congratulations!

You did it.

Yay!!

Thompson Flexibility Studies has 3 volumes.

You just completed Vol. I. Go ahead and catch your breath. Run around the block a few times. Jump up and down. Heck, do a little dance. Maybe even go treat yourself to your favorite food or dessert.

After you have celebrated, it is time to get back on the horse and keep riding.

The name of that horse is Vol. II in the Thompson Lip Flexibility Studies Intermediate version.

There is a lot more action and a lot more fun to be had in Vol. II so when you are ready, I will see you there.

All the best,

Kurt Thompson

# Thank You!

I want to personally thank you for participating in Vol. I from the Thompson Flexibility Studies. I sincerely hope this trumpet study provided a lot of value for you. If it did and you got something positive from this book, would you take 1 minute of your time and leave a great review from wherever you purchased it? If you purchased it at Trumpetsizzle.com, there is a review section where you can rate and review. Most of the online book sellers also have a section where you can rate and review.

In the unlikely event that you did not like this book, could you please tell me why before leaving any type of negative review? You can give me your comment and critique by emailing it to me: kurt@trumpetsizzle.com. I will take all comments seriously as there is always the possibility of a 2nd edition. Of course, the 2nd edition would take your comments and improve upon the original version.

I have truly done my best to ensure this book was worthy of your time and the money you invested.
You have a lot of books and instructional material to choose from and I sincerely want to thank you for flying with Trumpetsizzle.com, The *Trumpet Bliss* Series and The Thompson Flexibility Studies book!

www.ingramcontent.com/pod-product-compliance
Lightning Source LLC
Chambersburg PA
CBHW080845120626
46553CB00009B/2577